Gooseberry Patch co.

SO-CFB-106

country
Quick & Easy 2

Homestyle recipes
for serving
up hearty,
scrumptious meals
in a jiffy!

A Country Store In Your Mailbox®

Gooseberry Patch
600 London Road
P.O. Box 190
Delaware, OH 43015

www.gooseberrypatch.com
1·800·854·6673

Copyright 2006, Gooseberry Patch 1-931890-90-0
First Printing, May, 2006

Do you have a tried & true recipe...
tip, craft or memory that you'd like to see featured in a **Gooseberry
Patch** book? Visit our website at **www.gooseberrypatch.com**, register
and follow the easy steps to submit your favorite family recipe.
Or send them to us at:

Gooseberry Patch
Attn: Book Dept.
P.O. Box 190
Delaware, OH 43015

Don't forget to include the number of servings your recipe makes,
plus your name, street address, phone number and e-mail address.
If we select your recipe, your name will appear right along with
it...and you'll receive a **FREE** copy of the book!

table of Contents

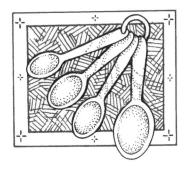

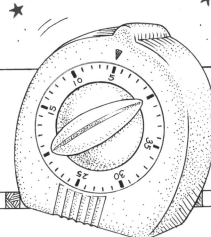

Dedication

For everyone who loves sitting down to a delicious meal with family...no matter how busy the day!

Appreciation

Heartfelt thanks to all our friends...we can always count on you to share the tastiest recipes!

munchies & More

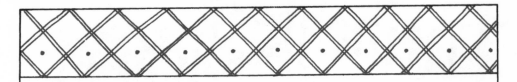

Garlic Potato Skins

Charmie Fisher
Fontana, CA

A restaurant favorite that's just as tasty at home.

6 russet potatoes
4 to 6 cloves garlic, minced
1/3 c. olive oil
Optional: shredded Monterey
    Jack or Cheddar cheese

coarse salt to taste
Garnish: sour cream, salsa,
    guacamole, chili, sliced
    green onion, cooked and
    crumbled bacon

Pierce potatoes all over with a fork. Bake on oven rack at 375 degrees until tender, about 55 minutes. Set aside to cool. Combine garlic and oil in a small saucepan over medium heat; sauté until garlic sizzles, about 2 minutes. Reduce heat; cook until garlic is tender, about 10 minutes. Let cool. Halve potatoes lengthwise and gently scoop out insides, leaving about 1/2-inch shells intact. Reserve baked potato for another recipe. Cut potato halves in half lengthwise; brush with garlic mixture and turn until completely coated. Arrange skin-side up on a baking sheet. Bake at 500 degrees for 7 minutes. Turn over; sprinkle with shredded cheese, if desired. Bake an additional 8 minutes; sprinkle immediately with salt. Top with desired toppings. Makes 2 dozen.

A cheery touch at the front door...fill a child-size wheelbarrow with pots of blooming golden marigolds.

munchies & More

Savory Stuffed Mushrooms

Marlene Kroll
Chicago, IL

I've been serving this appetizer to guests for years. Keep lots of copies of the recipe on hand...you'll get requests!

8 mushroom caps
1/4 c. butter, melted
2 cloves garlic, minced
1/4 c. shredded mozzarella
   cheese

2 T. white wine or chicken broth
1 t. soy sauce
1/3 c. thin wheat crackers,
   crushed
1 t. dried parsley

Dip mushroom caps in butter to coat; arrange in a lightly greased 8"x8" baking pan. Combine any remaining butter, garlic, cheese, wine or broth and soy sauce; stir well. Blend in cracker crumbs and parsley; spoon into mushrooms. Broil for about 5 minutes, or until golden. Makes 8.

Cover a bulletin board with pretty fabric and criss-cross with ribbons tacked in place...nice for showing off photos of good times with good friends. Simply slip the photos under the ribbons...easy!

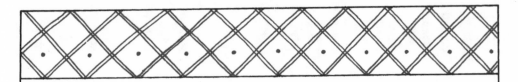

Tex-Mex Appetizer Tart

Linda Engeseth
Newhall, CA

*A savory combination of Mexican flavors. Try using
refried black beans for a yummy variation.*

8-1/2 oz. pkg. corn muffin mix
3/4 c. refried beans
1/2 c. salsa
1 c. shredded Cheddar cheese

Garnish: chopped lettuce,
chopped tomatoes, sliced
green onion, sliced black
olives, sour cream

Prepare corn muffin mix according to package directions; bake at
350 degrees in a greased 9" round tart pan. Set aside. Mix beans
with salsa; spread over warm corn muffin crust. Sprinkle with cheese;
return to oven. Bake at 350 degrees until cheese melts and beans are
heated through. Layer with lettuce, tomatoes, onion and olives;
top with sour cream. Cut into wedges to serve. Serves 6 to 8.

Favorite old game boards make whimsical settings for game
night buffets! Check the closet for forgotten games or pick
some up at yard sales. Cover with self-adhesive clear plastic
for wipe-clean ease.

munchies & More

Hearty Slow-Cooker Bean Dip

Mandy Cluck
McAlisterville, PA

Do you like it hot? Add a few drops of hot pepper sauce!

1 lb. ground beef
1-1/4 oz. pkg. taco
   seasoning mix
4-oz. can diced green
   chiles, drained
2 16-oz. cans refried beans

2 14-1/2 oz. cans diced
   tomatoes, drained
16-oz. pkg. pasteurized
   process cheese spread,
   cubed
tortilla chips

Brown ground beef and seasoning mix together in a skillet; drain.
Pour into a slow cooker; add remaining ingredients except tortilla
chips and mix well. Cover and cook on low setting for one to 2 hours,
stirring occasionally. Serve with tortilla chips. Serves 6 to 8.

Nothing makes a room cozier than big fluffy pillows! Look for
pillows in a variety of colors and textures...nestle them on sofas,
easy chairs and window alcoves.

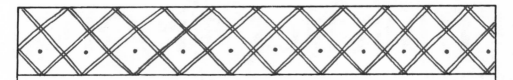

Green Olive-Cheese Puffs

Staci Meyers
Cocoa, FL

Guests will love these cheesy bites with a surprise inside!

8-oz. pkg. shredded sharp
   Cheddar cheese
1/2 c. butter, softened

1 c. all-purpose flour
7-oz. jar green olives with
   pimentos, drained

Combine cheese and butter in a blender or food processor; blend until smooth. Place in a mixing bowl; add flour and mix well. Roll out to 1/4-inch thickness; cut into forty-eight, 2"x2" squares. Wrap each square around an olive, sealing seams. Arrange on an ungreased baking sheet; bake at 400 degrees for 10 to 15 minutes, until golden. Makes 4 dozen.

Top glasses of fizzy lemon-lime soda with a scoop of sherbet...a refreshing treat on a hot day!

munchies & More

Hot Sausage Balls

Joanne Ostlund
Cuyahoga Falls, OH

So tasty, yet easy enough for a child to make!

10-oz. pkg. shredded sharp
  Cheddar cheese

1 lb. ground hot sausage
2 c. biscuit baking mix

Mix together cheese, sausage and baking mix. Roll into 1-1/2 inch balls; arrange on an ungreased jelly-roll pan. Bake for 20 minutes at 400 degrees. Makes 2 dozen.

Vintage Mason jars are ideal for storing small items all through the house...buttons, bobbins and thread spools in the sewing room or guest soaps and cotton balls in the bath. Top jar lids with a circle of calico for country charm.

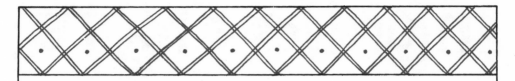

Pizza Dippers

Angela Evans
Johnston, IA

When I was a little girl, my mother always made these as a New Year's Eve treat. We would eat special food, watch movies and just enjoy being together.

2 c. all-purpose flour
1/4 c. grated Parmesan cheese
1 t. salt
2/3 c. shortening

1/2 lb. ground Italian sausage, browned and drained
1/3 c. plus 1 T. cold water

Combine flour, cheese and salt in a mixing bowl; cut in shortening until mixture is the size of small peas. Stir in browned sausage. Add water a little at a time, tossing and stirring with a fork until dough is just moist enough to hold together. Shape into one-inch balls; arrange on an ungreased baking sheet. Bake at 450 degrees for 10 to 12 minutes, until golden. Serve hot with warm Pizza Sauce for dipping. Makes 15 to 25.

Pizza Sauce:

8-oz. can tomato sauce
2 T. grated Parmesan cheese
1 T. oil

1/4 t. dried oregano
1/4 t. garlic salt
1/4 t. salt

Combine all ingredients in a small saucepan. Heat to boiling; reduce heat and simmer about 5 minutes.

The greatest sweetener of human life is friendship.

−Joseph Addison

munchies & More

Slow-Cooker Cheese Dip

Shellye McDaniel
De Kalb, TX

*This is a scrumptious chip dip...delicious spooned
over baked potatoes too!*

1 lb. ground beef
1 onion, chopped
1 clove garlic, chopped
8-oz. pkg. cream cheese, cubed
2 16-oz. pkgs. pasteurized
    process cheese spread, cubed
1/2 c. sour cream
1/2 c. evaporated milk
10-3/4 oz. can cream of
    mushroom soup
13-1/4 oz. can sliced
    mushrooms, drained
1 t. Worcestershire sauce
corn chips

Brown beef, onion and garlic in a skillet over medium heat; drain
well and set aside. Combine cheeses, sour cream, evaporated milk,
soup and mushrooms in a slow cooker; cover and cook on high setting
for one to 2 hours. Once cheese has melted, add Worcestershire and
meat mixture; stir well. Turn slow cooker down to low setting until
ready to serve. Serve with corn chips. Serves 6 to 8.

Give an old metal locker a
new life as a handy
mini-pantry for kitchen
staples or party
supplies...simply paint in a
soft country color.

PARTY SUPPLIES

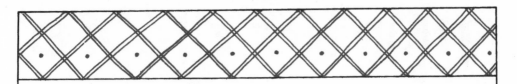

Bacon-Cheddar Appetizer

Lora Bohannon
Spanish Fork, UT

Our 2 favorite flavors together on a cracker.

8-oz. pkg. shredded sharp
   Cheddar cheese
3 T. onion, chopped
1/2 c. bacon bits

1/2 c. mayonnaise
9-1/2 oz. pkg. shredded wheat
   crackers

Blend together all ingredients except crackers. Arrange crackers on a baking sheet; top each with about one teaspoon of mixture. Place under a heated broiler for about 2 minutes, until cheese has melted. Makes 5 dozen.

Layered fabrics are warm and inviting around the house.
Try sweet lace toppers draped over tablecloths or thick
fluffy towels hung one over another.

munchies & More

Ham & Cheese Crescent Snacks

Coleen Lambert
Casco, WI

These can be made ahead and refrigerated up to 2 hours before baking...simply assemble, then cover with plastic wrap.

8-oz. tube refrigerated
   crescent rolls
2 T. butter, softened
1 t. mustard

1 c. cooked ham, diced
1/3 c. onion, chopped
1/3 c. green pepper, chopped
1 c. shredded Cheddar cheese

Unroll dough onto an ungreased baking sheet. Press into a 13"x9" rectangle, sealing perforations. Pinch edges to form a rim; set aside. Combine butter and mustard in a small bowl; mix well. Spread butter mixture over dough; sprinkle with ham, onion and green pepper. Bake at 375 degrees for 18 to 25 minutes, until edges are golden. Cut into squares; serve warm. Makes 2 dozen.

Wrap up hot rolls in a brightly colored bandanna...they'll stay toasty warm in the bread basket.

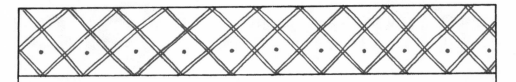

Double Deviled Eggs

Sharon Crider
Lebanon, MO

Devilishly good!

8 eggs, hard-boiled, peeled
   and halved
1/4 c. mayonnaise
1 t. onion juice
1 t. mustard

1/2 t. steak sauce
2-1/4 oz. can deviled ham
1/8 t. pepper
Garnish: fresh parsley sprigs

Place egg yolks in a bowl; set egg white halves aside. Mash yolks with mayonnaise, onion juice, mustard and steak sauce until smooth. Stir in ham and pepper; mix well. Spoon mixture into egg white halves; garnish each with a sprig of parsley. Chill for 30 minutes before serving. Makes 16.

Use vintage wallpaper scraps to make covers for
favorite books, then stamp on titles with fun rubber stamps.
Stack on bookshelves for vintage appeal.

Munchies & More

Bacon-Wrapped Sausages

Karen Asplund
Stillwater, MN

When I make these for the holidays, I have to triple the recipe because my family goes crazy for them!

1 lb. bacon, halved
1-lb. pkg. mini smoked
   sausages

1/2 c. brown sugar, packed

Roll a halved bacon slice around each sausage; arrange on an ungreased baking sheet. Sprinkle brown sugar over top and refrigerate for 4 hours or overnight. Bake at 350 degrees until golden, about 30 minutes. Makes 4 dozen.

A mini photo album is just right for keeping tried & true recipes handy on the kitchen counter. Slide in a few snapshots of happy family mealtimes too!

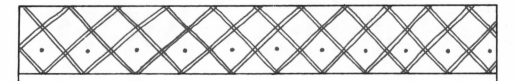

Spinach-Stuffed Mushrooms

Shirlee Dombrowski
Concord, CA

An unusual mushroom filling that's ready in no time at all.

12-oz. pkg. frozen spinach
    soufflé
16-oz. pkg. mushrooms, stems
    removed and chopped

1 c. shredded Parmesan cheese

Prepare soufflé according to package directions. Add mushroom stems to soufflé; mix well. Stuff mushroom caps with spinach mixture; top with cheese. Arrange on a lightly greased baking sheet; bake at 350 degrees for 10 to 15 minutes, or until cheese melts. Makes about 2 dozen.

Button, button, who's got the button? Search Grandma's
button box for intriguing buttons and hot glue them onto
small round magnets...sweet for hanging up children's artwork
and school papers!

munchies & More

Mini Sausage Tarts

Wanda Boykin
Lewisburg, TN

These look so fancy on an appetizer tray. Your friends will never know how easy they are...that's your little secret!

1 lb. ground sausage, browned
  and drained
8-oz. pkg. shredded Mexican-
  blend cheese

1 c. ranch salad dressing
2 T. black olives, chopped
4 pkgs. 15-count frozen
  mini phyllo cups

Combine sausage, cheese, salad dressing and olives; divide between phyllo cups. Arrange cups on an ungreased baking sheet; bake at 350 degrees for 10 to 12 minutes. Makes 5 dozen.

Pick up a glass garden cloche for delightful dining room displays...a basket of colored eggs nestled in Easter grass in springtime or a dear old Santa at Christmas.

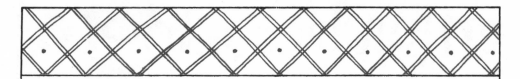

All-American Snack Mix

Jane Hutfles
Omaha, NE

The slow cooker does all the work! For variety, reduce the
cereals to 3 cups each and add 3 cups of corn chips.

4 c. bite-size crispy wheat
    cereal squares
4 c. doughnut-shaped oat cereal
3 c. thin pretzel sticks
12-oz. can salted peanuts

1/4 c. butter, melted
2 T. grated Parmesan cheese
1 t. garlic powder
1 t. celery salt
1/2 t. seasoned salt

Combine cereals, pretzels and nuts in a large bowl. Set aside. Combine
remaining ingredients in a medium bowl; pour over cereal mixture and
toss until mixed. Pour into a large slow cooker. Cover and cook on low
setting for 2-1/2 hours, stirring every 30 minutes. Uncover and cook
for an additional 30 minutes. Store in an airtight container.
Makes 3 quarts.

A simple solution to picnic pests...fit circles of tulle into wooden
embroidery hoops, then set them over the tops of pitchers and
serving bowls.

munchies & More

Chicken Feed Snack Mix

Kim Gludt
Anaheim, CA

Bet you can't stop nibbling on these savory crackers.

2 11-oz. pkgs. oyster crackers
1-oz. pkg. ranch salad dressing
   mix
1/2 t. dill weed

1/2 t. garlic powder
1/2 t. lemon pepper
1 c. corn oil

Place crackers in a large plastic zipping bag; combine remaining ingredients and pour over crackers. Let stand overnight, turning bag occasionally. Makes about 24 servings.

Give the fireplace a warm glow in summer...put away the fire screen, then set a big terra cotta pot of flame-colored zinnias or mums in the opening.

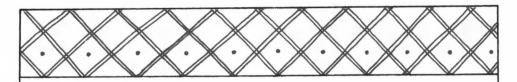

Hot Artichoke Dip

Marie Ludwick
Meredith, NH

A delicious way to serve artichokes.

14-oz. can artichokes, drained
   and chopped
1 c. grated Parmesan cheese
1/2 c. mayonnaise

1/2 c. sour cream
1 clove garlic, minced
bagel chips, shredded
   wheat crackers

Combine all ingredients except chips and crackers; spoon into a lightly greased 13"x9" baking pan. Bake at 350 degrees for 30 minutes, until hot and bubbly. Serve with chips and crackers. Serves 4 to 6.

Fill up a big party tray with fresh veggies for dipping and snacking...calorie-counting friends will thank you! Any extras can be tossed into a crunchy salad the next day.

munchies & More

Veggie Tortilla Pinwheels

Jamie Kehres
Findlay, OH

Substitute low-fat or fat-free cream cheese, if you like...these tasty treats will be just as creamy and good.

8-oz. pkg. cream cheese, softened
1-oz. pkg. ranch salad dressing mix
2-1/4 oz. pkg. dried beef, chopped
1/2 c. broccoli, chopped
1/2 c. cauliflower, chopped
1/4 c. green onion, chopped
1/4 c. green olives with pimentos, chopped
5 8-inch flour tortillas
Garnish: salsa

Combine cream cheese and dressing mix in a mixing bowl; stir in beef and vegetables. Spread evenly over tortillas; roll tightly and wrap in plastic wrap. Chill for at least 2 hours; unwrap and cut into 1/2-inch slices. Serve with salsa. Makes about 2-1/2 dozen.

A family recipe book is a wonderful way to preserve one generation's traditions for the next. Ask everyone to share their most-requested recipes, just the way they make them. Arrange typed or handwritten recipes into a book and have enough copies made for everyone!

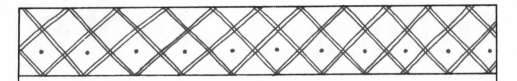

Crabby Dip

Susan Fracker
New Concord, OH

Guests will feel happy, not crabby, when they scoop up this dip!

1-1/2 c. cream cheese, softened
2 T. onion, grated
1 T. Worcestershire sauce
1 T. lemon juice
1/8 t. salt

6-oz. can crabmeat, drained
1 c. cocktail sauce
Optional: lemon pepper to taste
round buttery crackers or
    shredded wheat crackers

Blend first 5 ingredients and spread onto a serving platter. Sprinkle with crabmeat. Top with cocktail sauce; cover. Chill for at least 4 hours. Sprinkle with lemon pepper to taste, if desired. Serve with crackers. Serves 6 to 8.

Fill up glass hurricane shades with seashells, beach pebbles, tiny pine cones or other natural items gathered during leisurely walks...a simple reminder of family time spent together.

munchies & More

Creamy Cucumber Bites

Charissa Stiefvater
Schaumburg, IL

My best friend, Jenny, gave me this recipe several years ago.
Now I can't have a get-together without it!

8-oz. pkg. cream cheese,
   softened
1/2 c. mayonnaise
1-oz. pkg. ranch salad dressing
   mix

1/2 t. dill weed
1 loaf sliced party rye bread
1 cucumber, thinly sliced
Garnish: dill weed

Combine cream cheese, mayonnaise, dressing mix and dill weed in
a medium bowl; mix well and spread on one side of each bread slice.
Top each with a slice of cucumber and sprinkle with additional dill
weed. Chill until ready to serve. Makes 2 dozen.

Old-fashioned teacups are perfect for mini flower
arrangements...just the right size for a bathroom counter or
dressing table.

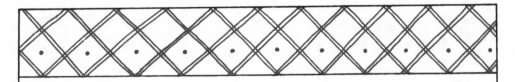

Snappy Chicken Balls

Brenda Hughes
Houston, TX

My favorite gift shop always serves these delicious finger foods at its holiday open house.

2 c. cooked chicken, finely
   chopped
1-1/2 c. almonds, finely chopped
1/4 c. chutney, chopped
1 T. green onion, finely chopped
8-oz. pkg. cream cheese,
   softened

1/4 c. mayonnaise
2 t. curry powder
salt to taste
1 c. sweetened flaked coconut

Combine chicken, almonds, chutney and onion; mix well and set aside. In a separate bowl, blend cream cheese, mayonnaise, curry powder and salt. Combine chicken mixture and cream cheese mixture; chill. Shape into bite-size balls; roll each in coconut. Arrange on serving trays; cover and refrigerate up to 3 days, until serving time. Makes about 6-1/2 dozen.

Dress up the front porch with wicker chairs, baskets of flowers and a big wreath on the front door...let friends & family know you're glad to see them!

munchies & More

Buffalo Tenders

Deb Lange
Williamson, NY

A tasty, easy-to-eat twist on Buffalo-style chicken wings.

2 lbs. boneless, skinless chicken
   breast, cut into strips
1/2 to 1 c. all-purpose flour
oil for frying

1/2 c. hot pepper sauce
Garnish: blue cheese salad
   dressing

Roll chicken strips in flour. Heat oil in a skillet over medium heat; fry strips until golden on both sides. Drain strips and place in a large plastic zipping bag. Sprinkle pepper sauce over strips and shake until well-coated. Serve with blue cheese dressing for dipping. Makes 6 to 8 servings.

Mismatched dining table chairs from the flea market are easily pulled together with matching paint. Stitch up some seat cushions from tea towels in the prettiest prints...how clever!

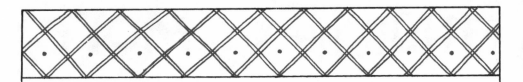

Holiday Tortilla Chips

Amy Wolfe
Marysville, WA

*Perfect for any holiday! Pick up some veggie-flavored tortillas
for colorful chips...cut out ghosts and pumpkins for
Halloween and snowmen for Christmas.*

3 12-oz. pkgs. flour tortillas Garnish: Mexican dip or salsa
salt to taste

Cut tortillas into shapes using 3" to 4" cookie cutters. Spray each
shape lightly with non-stick vegetable spray. Arrange on a baking
sheet sprayed with non-stick vegetable spray and sprinkle with salt.
Bake at 350 degrees for 5 to 7 minutes, or until edges are golden.
Remove to a wire rack to cool. Serve with Mexican dip or salsa.
Makes 4 to 6 cups.

Want to catch up with friends, but don't have a lot
of time for home cooking? Have a potluck! Ask
each friend to prepare a special recipe...everyone can relax
and spend a carefree evening together.

munchies & More

Pepperoni Bread

Cheryl Lagler
Zionsville, PA

We enjoy this for dinner with a tossed salad...it
makes dinner-size portions for 6 people.

16-oz. loaf frozen bread dough,
   thawed
1 egg
garlic powder and dried oregano
   to taste
4-oz. pkg. turkey pepperoni
   slices

1/2 c. shredded sharp Cheddar
   cheese
1/4 c. shredded mozzarella
   cheese
Garnish: pizza sauce

Roll bread dough out into a rectangle 1/2-inch thick on a floured
surface; set aside. Beat egg with garlic powder and oregano; brush
half the egg mixture on dough. Arrange pepperoni edge-to-edge on
dough; top with cheeses. Roll up and cut in half; pinch edges and
place seam-side down on a lightly greased baking sheet. Brush tops
with remaining egg mixture. Bake at 350 degrees for 20 to
25 minutes. Serve with warm pizza sauce. Makes 12 servings.

Mount a wrought iron curtain rod over the
stove, then use S-hooks to hang up pots and
pans...so convenient!

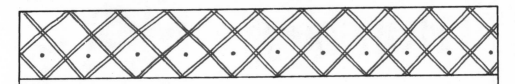

Swedish Meatballs

Kimberly Carruthers
Canastota, NY

This is my grandmother's recipe. It's been a part of our traditional Christmas Eve dinner since my mom was a child. I always look forward to Christmas Eve because of these meatballs!

2 lbs. ground beef
1 egg
1/3 c. bread crumbs
1 t. allspice

10-3/4 oz. can cream of
    mushroom soup
3/4 c. milk

Combine ground beef, egg, bread crumbs and allspice; mix well. Form into one-inch balls. Brown in a skillet over medium heat; drain. Combine soup and milk; pour over meatballs in skillet. Cover and simmer over low heat for 30 minutes. Makes 6 servings.

Freeze meatballs individually, then simply pop them into a plastic egg carton. Later you can remove just the number you need...easy!

munchies & More

Creamy Horseradish Ham Rolls

Vickie

The bite of the horseradish is balanced by the smoothness of the cream cheese.

2 8-oz. pkgs. cream cheese, softened
3 green onions, chopped

5 t. prepared horseradish
4 8-oz. pkgs. sliced cooked ham

Mix cream cheese, onions and horseradish together; spread onto ham slices. Roll up; slice each roll into 4 pieces. Secure with toothpicks; refrigerate until serving. Makes 5 to 6-1/2 dozen.

Line a pretty basket with a vintage hankerchief, fill with mini toiletries and place in the guest bath...a home-away-from-home welcome for overnight visitors.

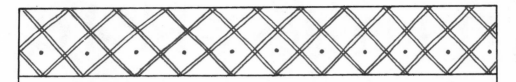

Chinese Chicken Wings

Suzanne Erickson
Columbus, OH

A must-have for the game-day appetizer table!

2 to 3 lbs. chicken wings
1/2 c. soy sauce
1 c. pineapple juice
1/3 c. brown sugar, packed

1 t. ground ginger
1 t. garlic salt
1/2 t. pepper

Place wings in a large plastic zipping bag; set aside. Combine remaining ingredients and pour over wings, turning to coat. Refrigerate for 12 to 24 hours, turning several times. Drain wings, discarding marinade; arrange in a single layer on an ungreased jelly-roll pan. Bake at 450 degrees for 45 minutes, until golden and juices run clear when pierced. Makes 2 to 2-1/2 dozen.

Cans with colorful labels make clever holders for tableware at informal gatherings. Look for them in the import section of the grocery store.

munchies & More

Easy Sweet-and-Sour Meatballs

Lynn Fazz
Yuma, AZ

*A quick & easy appetizer for guests and potlucks...keep it
warm by serving right from the slow cooker.*

2-lb. pkg. frozen meatballs,
    thawed
16-oz. can pineapple tidbits

18-oz. bottle barbecue sauce
Optional: 1 onion and
    1 green pepper, diced

Combine all ingredients in a slow cooker. Cover and cook on low
setting for one hour. Serves 8 to 10.

Pour hot tea into ice cube trays, drop in mini lemon wedges, then
freeze. They'll keep iced tea cold without watering it down.

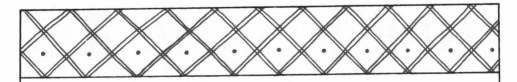

Best-Ever Clam Dip

Mavis Peterson
Moline, IL

Mmm...we can almost smell the ocean breeze!

1 clove garlic, halved
8-oz. pkg. cream cheese,
   softened
4 to 5 T. clam broth
7-1/2 oz. can minced clams,
   drained

2 t. lemon juice
1-1/2 t. Worcestershire sauce
1/2 t. salt
1/8 t. pepper
assorted crackers

Rub a mixing bowl with garlic; discard garlic. Add remaining
ingredients to bowl and mix well. Chill. Serve with crackers.
Makes about 3 cups.

Turn a metal cookie sheet into a
family message center...spray on
craft paint in a cheerful color.
Attach a ribbon hanger and use
magnets to hold notes
and reminders.

Aunt Judy's Dill Dip

Shawna Denney
Cloudcroft, NM

When I was growing up, my best friend, Barb, and I did everything together with each other's family. This recipe is one that Barb's Aunt Judy used to fix for large family gatherings. It always reminds me of picnics and warm summer evenings.

2 c. sour cream
1 T. lemon juice
3 T. dried parsley
1-1/2 T. dill weed

2 t. dried sage
1 t. dried, minced garlic
1 round loaf pumpernickel
　　or rye bread

Mix together all ingredients except bread; chill. Cut a round hole in top of loaf; hollow out center. Surround loaf with torn bread pieces; fill with dip. Makes about 2-1/3 cups.

Use new terra cotta pots as whimsical containers for dips and spreads. Simply line with plastic wrap or set plastic containers inside, then tuck in a new plant stake with the recipe name written on it.

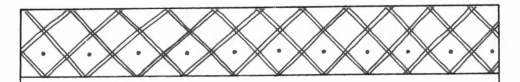

Mom's Tasty Kielbasa

Jackie McBride
Barnesville, OH

My mom, Sharon Doty, made this for my wedding reception.
She's had the recipe so long that her copy is faded...it has
a sweet-and-sour taste that's so delicious.

1 c. onion, sliced
1 c. celery, chopped
1 to 2 T. butter
1/2 c. catsup
1 t. Worcestershire sauce
1/4 c. vinegar

1/4 c. sugar
1 T. mustard
1 t. paprika
1 lb. Kielbasa, cut into
   1-inch pieces

In a skillet over medium heat, sauté onion and celery in butter until tender. Mix together remaining ingredients except Kielbasa. Mix well, then add Kielbasa; bring to a boil. Reduce heat to medium and cook until sauce thickens, stirring often. Makes 8 to 10.

Slip children's artwork between 2 pieces of clear self-adhesive
plastic for placemats that are both practical and playful!

munchies & More

Favorite Beef & Cheese Ball

Lori Lenz
Bluford, IL

Try rolling this cheese ball in coarse black pepper,
minced parsley or finely chopped nuts.

2 8-oz. pkgs. cream cheese,
   softened
2 t. flavor enhancer
1 t. Worcestershire sauce

2-1/2 oz. pkg. dried beef,
   minced
4 green onions, chopped
assorted crackers

Combine all ingredients except crackers; chill for several minutes.
Form into a ball. Serve with crackers. Makes 12 to 15 servings.

Macadamia Nut Dip

Judy Borecky
Escondido, CA

Spoon into a pineapple half for your next luau party.

8-oz. pkg. cream cheese,
   softened
1/2 c. sour cream
1 c. macadamia nuts, chopped

2 T. prepared horseradish
2 green onions, minced
1/8 t. garlic salt
assorted crackers

Mix all ingredients together except crackers; chill. Serve with crackers.
Makes 6 to 10 servings.

A smiling face is
half the meal.

—Latvian Proverb

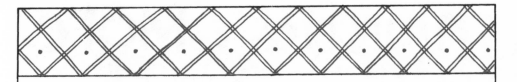

Salmon Roll

Angela Nichols
Mount Airy, NC

We like to serve this with water crackers.

16-oz. can salmon,
   drained and flaked
8-oz. pkg. cream cheese,
   softened
1 T. lemon juice

2 T. onion, chopped
1 t. horseradish sauce
1/4 t. salt
Garnish: chopped nuts
assorted crackers

Combine all ingredients except nuts and crackers; shape into a roll. Roll in nuts; chill. Serve with crackers. Makes 12 to 15 servings.

Plant lots of old-fashioned cutting flowers like zinnias, snapdragons, cosmos, pinks and cornflowers. They'll bloom for you twice...first in the garden, then again when cut and brought into the house.

Fresh & Tasty

Cucumber Freezer Salad

Dawn Psik
Aliquippa, PA

This makes a light refreshing side dish for a picnic or barbecue on a warm summer evening. It's great if you have lots of cucumbers growing in your garden.

2 c. sugar
1 c. cider vinegar
1 t. salt
1 t. celery seed
7 c. cucumbers, sliced

1 green pepper, sliced
1 red pepper, sliced
3 onions, sliced and separated
    into rings

In a 2-quart saucepan, whisk together sugar, vinegar, salt and celery seed. Bring to a boil; boil for one minute. Let cool; set aside. In a large bowl, combine remaining ingredients; pour cooled liquid over top. Toss to coat; divide among 4 freezer bags. Freeze. To serve, allow bags to thaw for one to 2 hours at room temperature. Makes 6 to 8 servings.

Arrange small dolls, pull toys and other well-loved playthings on a hallway table for a sweet reminder of childhood.

Claremont Salad

Linda Day
Wall, NJ

A crisp make-ahead cabbage salad that's an old diner tradition.

1 head cabbage, shredded
2 green peppers, sliced
2 cucumbers, peeled and sliced

2 carrots, peeled and sliced
1 onion, sliced

Mix all ingredients together. Toss with dressing; refrigerate overnight. Serves 6 to 8.

Dressing:

1 c. white vinegar
1/3 c. water
1/2 c. oil

3/4 c. sugar
1 T. salt
2 t. garlic, minced

Mix all ingredients together.

Ripe red tomatoes and sweet onions from the farmers' market are such a treat in summer...serve them simply, with just a dash of oil & vinegar and a sprinkle of fresh basil.

Southwestern Layered Salad

Tonya Sheppard
Galveston, TX

Perfect for potlucks and family gatherings.

8-oz. container sour cream
3-oz. pkg. cream cheese,
  softened
10-oz. can tomatoes with
  chiles, drained
1 t. ground cumin
4 c. romaine lettuce, shredded
2 to 3 tomatoes, chopped
15-oz. can black beans, rinsed
  and drained

15-oz. can corn, drained
1 sweet red onion, chopped
15-oz. can pinto beans,
  rinsed and drained
2 red peppers, chopped
Garnish: shredded sharp
  Cheddar cheese, chopped
  green onion

Combine sour cream, cream cheese, tomatoes with chiles and cumin in a blender; process until smooth. Chill. Layer vegetables in order given among eight, one-pint Mason jars. Spoon sour cream mixture over top; sprinkle with shredded cheese and green onion. Cover and chill for one hour. Makes 8 servings.

Dress up dining room chairs in a flash...simply slide patterned pillowcases over the backs. Tie a contrasting cord around the top of each chair with a tassel hanging down the chair back.

Mother's Cornbread Salad

Betty Hickey
Smithville, TN

*Mom always used her wonderful home-grown
tomatoes in this family recipe.*

2 lbs. tomatoes, chopped
1 c. onion, chopped
1 c. green pepper, chopped
1 c. sweet pickle, chopped
1 c. mayonnaise
1/2 c. sweet pickle juice

1 T. sugar
1 lb. bacon, crisply cooked
  and crumbled, divided
2 8-1/2 oz. pkgs. corn muffin
  mix, prepared and cubed

Mix tomatoes, onion, pepper and pickle in a bowl; set aside.
In a separate bowl, mix mayonnaise, pickle juice, sugar and half the
bacon. Place half the cornbread in an ungreased 13"x9" baking pan.
Top with half the tomato mixture and half the mayonnaise mixture.
Repeat layering and top with remaining bacon. Serves 12 to 16.

Just for fun, turn vintage jelly glasses into candles.
Holding a wick in place, pour scented wax gel into each glass.
They're especially pretty with gels in glowing "jelly" colors like
red and amber!

Zucchini Zarinade

Kerri York
Spokane, WA

A tasty way to make use of a bumper crop of zucchini!

4 c. zucchini, thinly sliced
1 c. celery, thinly sliced
1/2 c. sliced mushrooms
1/2 c. sliced black olives
1/4 c. red pepper, chopped
1/4 c. green pepper, chopped

1 c. picante sauce or salsa
1/2 c. vinegar
3 T. olive oil
3 T. sugar
1/2 t. dried oregano
1 clove garlic, minced

Combine vegetables in a large mixing bowl; toss to mix and set aside. Combine remaining ingredients in a small bowl; whisk together and pour over vegetable mixture. Cover and chill for several hours, or overnight. Makes 6 to 8 servings.

Roast garlic is heavenly to spread on bread and so easy in the microwave! Slice the top off a whole garlic bulb and set it in a microwave-safe container. Sprinkle to taste with salt, pepper and olive oil, add a little water and cover with plastic wrap. Heat on high setting for 8 minutes, until soft.

Fresh & Tasty

Pizza Salad

Krista Smith
Dayton, OH

Try using shredded pizza-blend cheese too.

16-oz. pkg. rotini or bowtie
   pasta, uncooked
1 green pepper, chopped
1 red pepper, chopped
1 tomato, chopped
4 to 5 green onions, sliced
4-oz. can sliced mushrooms,
   drained
2-1/4 oz. can sliced black
   olives, drained

2-1/2 oz. pkg. sliced pepperoni
2 cloves garlic, minced
1 t. dried oregano
1/2 t. salt
1/4 t. pepper
8-oz. bottle Italian salad
   dressing
1 c. shredded mozzarella cheese
2 T. grated Parmesan cheese

Prepare pasta according to package directions; rinse with cold water and drain. Place pasta in a large serving bowl; mix in peppers, tomato, onions, mushrooms, olives and pepperoni. Add garlic, oregano, salt and pepper; toss well. Chill. At serving time, add dressing and cheeses; toss well. Serves 8 to 10.

A china sugar bowl makes a charming vase.
Place a block of floral foam inside and arrange
short-stemmed flowers in the foam.

North Shore Chicken Salad

Lori Mulhern
Rosemount, MN

*I can't tell you how many times I've shared this fabulous recipe
with dear friends & family. It may look complicated but
it really takes only a little time and effort.*

1 c. long-cooking wild rice,
   uncooked
2 14-1/2 oz. cans chicken broth
2 T. lemon juice
2 boneless, skinless chicken
   breasts, cooked and cubed
2 green onions, sliced

1/2 red pepper, diced
1/2 c. snow peas, cut into 1-inch
   pieces
1 avocado, cubed
1 c. toasted pecan halves,
   coarsely chopped

Cover rice with water in a bowl; let stand overnight. Drain. Bring
broth to a boil in a medium saucepan. Add rice; lower heat, cover
and simmer for 30 to 40 minutes, until tender and broth is absorbed.
Toss warm rice with lemon juice in a medium bowl; let cool. Add
chicken, onions, pepper, peas and Dijon Dressing; toss to coat. Cover
and refrigerate for 2 to 4 hours. At serving time, add avocado and
pecans; toss gently. Makes 8 to 10 servings.

Dijon Dressing:

1/3 c. oil
1/4 c. rice wine vinegar
1 T. Dijon mustard
1 t. garlic, minced

1/2 t. salt
1/4 t. pepper
1/4 t. sugar

Combine all ingredients in a food processor or bowl; blend thoroughly.

Need just a dash of lemon juice? Pierce the
lemon with an ice pick, squeeze out as
needed and return to the refrigerator
until next use.

Fresh & Tasty

Walnut & Feta Spinach Salad

Tiffanie Ansel
Luna Pier, MI

An extra-special salad that's just right with grilled chicken or steak.

2 c. raspberries
1/3 c. sugar
1/3 c. oil
2 T. cider vinegar
1/4 t. Worcestershire sauce

6-oz. pkg. baby spinach
1 sweet onion, thinly sliced and
   separated into rings
1/2 to 1 c. crumbled feta cheese
1/2 c. chopped walnuts

In a saucepan over medium heat, bring raspberries and sugar to a boil; cook for one minute. Strain juice and discard pulp. Combine raspberry juice with oil, vinegar and Worcestershire sauce in a blender; blend until smooth. Pour into a serving bowl; add remaining ingredients. Toss well. Makes 8 servings.

Redecorating with new curtains?
Buy a little extra fabric...make toss pillows and cover
lampshades to tie the whole room together.

Peppy Olive Salad

Stacie Allison
Fredericksburg, VA

*Try a spoonful of this salad as a topping on a sandwich
of sliced deli cold cuts...mmm!*

16-oz. jar green olives with
  pimentos, drained and
  chopped
6-oz. can black olives, drained
  and chopped
1 c. celery, chopped

12-oz. jar pepperoncini peppers,
  drained and chopped
6 cloves garlic, minced
1 T. dried oregano
1/2 c. olive oil
1/2 c. wine vinegar

Combine all ingredients in a serving bowl. Cover and refrigerate for at
least 2 days, stirring occasionally. Serves 6 to 8.

Bakery-fresh bread...easy! Thaw frozen dough,
roll out and sprinkle with minced garlic and chopped rosemary
or oregano. Roll up and bake as the package directs...mmm,
slice and pass the butter!

Rainbow Rotini Salad

Kathy Grashoff
Fort Wayne, IN

So colorful on a buffet table!

16-oz. pkg. rainbow rotini,
  cooked
2 tomatoes, chopped
1 green pepper, chopped
3/4 c. onion, chopped

3-1/2 oz. pkg. pepperoni,
  chopped
6-oz. can sliced black olives,
  drained
8-oz. pkg. crumbled feta cheese

Mix together all ingredients except cheese; toss with Herb Dressing.
Chill for at least 2 hours; add cheese. Serves 6 to 8.

Herb Dressing:

1/2 c. oil
2 T. vinegar
1 clove garlic, chopped
1/4 c. dried parsley

1 t. dried basil
1/2 t. dried oregano
2 t. salt
1/2 t. pepper

Combine all ingredients; mix well.

A vintage birdcage on a
stand makes a shabby
planter for a sunny corner.
Brighten it with
fresh white paint, then tuck
in pots of plants. Pull plant
fronds though the bars to
trail below.

Chickpea-Mushroom Salad

Tara Denney
Englewood, CO

A hearty, filling salad...spoon into red pepper cups
for a party presentation.

6 slices bacon
1 c. sliced mushrooms
1/4 c. lemon juice, divided
20-oz. can chickpeas, drained
    and rinsed
1/2 c. red onion, sliced
1 clove garlic, minced

2 T. fresh parsley, chopped
1/4 t. pepper
1/4 c. oil
1 c. tomatoes, chopped
1 c. seasoned croutons
romaine lettuce

In a skillet over medium heat, cook bacon until crisp. Remove and crumble bacon, leaving 2 tablespoons drippings in skillet. Sauté mushrooms in drippings; remove from heat. Stir in one tablespoon lemon juice; transfer to a bowl. Toss in chickpeas, bacon, onion, garlic, parsley and pepper; set aside. Combine remaining lemon juice and oil; stir into salad. Chill for one to 2 hours. At serving time, add tomatoes and croutons; toss lightly. Serve on lettuce leaves. Serves 4.

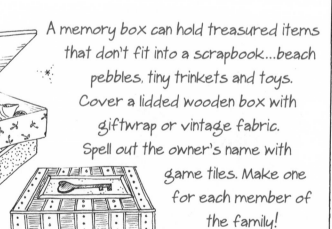

A memory box can hold treasured items that don't fit into a scrapbook...beach pebbles, tiny trinkets and toys. Cover a lidded wooden box with giftwrap or vintage fabric. Spell out the owner's name with game tiles. Make one for each member of the family!

Mom's Bean Salad

Jenny Lyn Day
Marceline, MO

I learned this recipe from my mother at a very young age...she always added her own special pickle relish.

15-1/2 oz. can kidney beans,
    drained and rinsed
2 eggs, hard-boiled, peeled
    and chopped
1/4 c. sweet onion, chopped

2 T. mayonnaise
Optional: 1/3 c. pickle relish
1 t. paprika
1/2 t. sugar

Combine all ingredients in a large bowl; mix well. Serve warm or cold.
Serves 4 to 6.

Pick up single salt & pepper shakers at tag sales...so useful for dispensing a shake of seasonings like cinnamon or chili powder right at the dining table.

German Potato Salad

Carla Urse
Columbus, OH

The perfect partner for grilled bratwurst!

10 slices bacon, cut crosswise
    into 1/4-inch pieces
3 lbs. new potatoes, boiled
    and diced
1 onion, chopped

1/2 t. sugar
3 T. cider vinegar, divided
3/4 c. beef broth
2 T. fresh parsley, chopped
salt and pepper to taste

Sauté bacon in a large skillet over medium heat until crisp.
Drain bacon on paper towels, reserving 3 tablespoons drippings in
skillet. Combine bacon and potatoes in a large bowl; keep warm.
Add onion to skillet and sauté over medium-high heat, stirring often,
for 3 minutes, until onion is transparent. Add sugar, 2 tablespoons
vinegar and broth; reduce to medium-low heat and simmer for
2 minutes. Add onion mixture and parsley to potato mixture. Toss
gently with remaining vinegar; sprinkle with salt and pepper. Serve
warm or at room temperature. Makes 8 to 10 servings.

Small birdhouses make whimsical toppers for garden fence
posts. Pick up several matching birdhouses at a craft store or
collect a variety of styles at flea markets.

Fresh & Tasty

Southern Macaroni Salad

Wendy Lee Paffenroth
Pine Island, NY

Everyone always wants seconds of this tasty salad!
A relative in Virginia shared it with me.

2 green peppers, chopped
3 tomatoes, chopped
1 onion, chopped
3 T. vinegar
1/4 c. sugar

1-3/4 T. celery seed
1-1/8 t. salt
1 c. mayonnaise
2 16-oz. pkgs. elbow macaroni,
   cooked

Mix first 7 ingredients together in a large bowl; let stand for
30 minutes. Stir in mayonnaise and macaroni; chill. Serves 12.

Don't toss away those old rubber boots...they make clever
planters! Trim them with stripes or dots cut from colored craft
tape, then fill with soil and potted flowers. Fun!

Farm Girl Salad

Nell Schneider
Sullivan, MO

Another delicious variation on layered salad...everyone loves it!

1 head lettuce, shredded
1 head cauliflower, chopped
1 red onion, chopped
1-1/2 c. mayonnaise

1 lb. bacon, crisply cooked
　and crumbled
1/4 c. grated Parmesan cheese
1/2 c. sugar

In a large bowl, layer ingredients in given order; refrigerate.
Stir before serving. Serves 8 to 10.

A tasty topping for baked potatoes...make your own yogurt
cheese. Spoon plain unsweetened yogurt into a cheesecloth-lined
colander and set it on a deep plate. Cover with plastic wrap and
refrigerate overnight. The next day, season the fresh cheese
with salt, pepper and dill or chives. Mmm!

Fresh & Tasty

The Best Coleslaw

Betty McGinty
Cleburne, TX

Try stirring in some mandarin oranges for added color and flavor.

3 c. cabbage, shredded
1/2 c. fresh parsley, chopped
1/2 c. green onion, chopped
2 to 3 T. sugar

3 T. vinegar
2 T. oil
1 t. salt

Mix cabbage, parsley and onion in a bowl; set aside. Combine sugar, vinegar, oil and salt; mix well. Pour over cabbage mixture; toss to coat. Serves 8 to 10.

Stack 2 cake stands to create a delightful and oh-so-easy centerpiece! Fill it with fresh fruits and small tumblers of flowers...pretty!

Chinese Cabbage Salad

Shirley Fair
Ontario, Canada

*Serve right away to enjoy the crunchy texture of the noodles
or chill first and let the noodles soften.*

1 head Chinese cabbage, sliced
6 green onions, sliced
1/2 c. margarine
1 c. sliced almonds
1/2 c. sesame seed
2 3-oz. pkgs. ramen noodles,
   crushed

Mix cabbage and onions together in a medium bowl; refrigerate overnight. Melt margarine in a skillet over medium heat. Add almonds, sesame seed and noodles, reserving seasoning packets for another recipe. Cook and stir until golden. Combine with cabbage mixture. Add Oriental Dressing just before serving; toss to coat. Serves 10.

Oriental Dressing:

1/2 c. olive oil
1/2 c. vinegar
1 T. plus 1 t. soy sauce
1 c. sugar

Combine all ingredients in a saucepan; heat until sugar is dissolved.

Bring cherished memories out of hiding! Have enlargements made of favorite photos...choose a theme like family trips or birthday parties. Group together in thrift-store frames all painted to match.

Fresh & Tasty

Popcorn Salad

Laura Pilquist
Stillwater, MN

While this is excellent for large gatherings, it's easy to halve the recipe if you're serving a smaller group.

12 c. popped popcorn
2 lbs. bacon, crisply cooked
    and crumbled
2 8-oz. pkgs. shredded
    Cheddar cheese

2 c. mayonnaise
2 c. celery, diced
2 c. sliced water chestnuts
2/3 c. green onion, chopped

Mix all ingredients together in a large bowl; serve immediately. Makes 18 to 24 servings.

Vintage-style souvenir tea towels make whimsical oversized napkins...handy for messy-but-tasty foods like barbecued ribs, corn on the cob and wedges of watermelon!

Broccoli-Cauliflower Toss

Sue Hohlen
Dixon, IL

Crispy, crunchy goodness!

5 c. broccoli flowerets
5 c. cauliflower flowerets
Optional: 1 onion, chopped
2 c. cherry tomatoes, halved
1 c. mayonnaise

1/2 c. sour cream
1 T. vinegar
2 T. sugar
salt and pepper to taste

Combine vegetables in a large bowl; set aside. Mix mayonnaise, sour cream, vinegar and sugar; pour over vegetables. Toss to coat; sprinkle with salt and pepper. Chill for 3 to 4 hours. Serves 10 to 12.

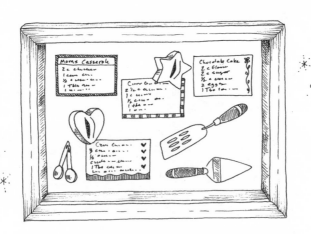

Family recipes make a memory-filled kitchen wall display. Arrange recipe cards or clippings in a shadowbox purchased at a craft store, adding cookie cutters and even mini kitchen utensils as you like. How about a snapshot of Mom rolling out her famous sugar cookies?

Warm & Wonderful Chicken Salad

Susan Fracker
New Concord, OH

*I first tried this years ago at a baby shower for a special friend.
It's perfect with fresh fruit and a warm muffin.*

2 c. boneless, skinless chicken
   breast, cooked and shredded
2 c. celery, diced
1 T. onion, grated
1 c. mayonnaise

1/2 c. slivered almonds
1/2 t. lemon juice
1-1/2 c. shredded Cheddar
   cheese, divided
1/2 c. potato chips, crushed

Mix chicken, celery, onion, mayonnaise, almonds, lemon juice and
one cup cheese in a greased 13"x9" baking pan. Top with remaining
cheese and chips. Bake at 450 degrees for 15 to 20 minutes.
Serves 6 to 8.

*Make cheese curls quickly for garnishing salads...simply pull a
vegetable peeler across the block of cheese.*

Creamy Squash Casserole

Melissa Cassulis
Cassville, NY

The creamy sauce and crunchy topping really set off the squash.

6 zucchini or yellow squash,
   thinly sliced
10-3/4 oz. can cream of
   chicken soup
1 c. sour cream

1/3 c. butter, softened
2 carrots, peeled and shredded
1/2 c. onion, finely chopped
2-3/4 c. herb-flavored stuffing
   mix, divided

Combine squash with a small amount of water in a saucepan; bring to
a boil for 3 minutes. Drain and set aside. In a large bowl, combine
soup, sour cream, butter, carrots and onion; stir in 2 cups stuffing mix.
Fold in squash; transfer to a greased 13"x9" baking pan. Sprinkle with
remaining stuffing mix. Bake, uncovered, at 350 degrees for
25 minutes. Makes 10 to 12 servings.

*It is amazing how much the little niceties of life have to do with
making a dinner pleasant.*
—Book of Etiquette by Lillian Eichler, 1921

Fresh & Tasty

Nutty Sweet Potato Casserole

Rosie Morris
Ruston, LA

Everybody's first choice at Thanksgiving dinner.

3 c. sweet potatoes, peeled,
   boiled and mashed
1/2 c. sugar
1 c. butter, melted and divided
1/2 c. milk

2 eggs, beaten
1 t. vanilla extract
1 c. brown sugar, packed
1/2 c. all-purpose flour
1 c. chopped pecans

Combine potatoes, sugar, 1/2 cup butter, milk, eggs and vanilla.
Mix well; spoon into a greased 13"x9" baking pan and set aside.
Mix remaining butter and other ingredients together; sprinkle over
potato mixture. Bake at 350 degrees for 25 minutes. Serves 10 to 12.

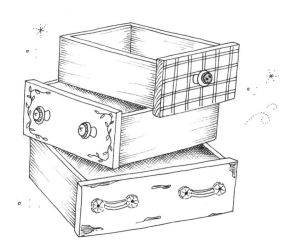

A quick way to give new personality to dressers or
vanities...just add new knobs! Look for vintage knobs at flea
markets, or give new knobs character by gluing on buttons,
bottle caps or other fanciful small objects.

Green Bean Delight

Jackie Balla
Walbridge, OH

An old standby dressed up with shredded cheese and nuts.

4 16-oz. cans green beans,
   drained
1-oz. pkg. ranch salad dressing
   mix
2 10-3/4 oz. cans cream of
   mushroom soup

1/4 c. milk
8-oz. pkg. shredded Colby Jack
   cheese
1 c. sliced almonds or cashews
2.8-oz. can French fried onions

Place green beans in a lightly greased 13"x9" baking pan; set aside.
Combine dressing mix, soup and milk in a small bowl; pour over
beans. Sprinkle with cheese and nuts; top with onions. Bake at
350 degrees for 25 minutes. Serves 8 to 10.

Trios of mesh hanging
baskets designed for
storing produce in the kitchen
make clever storage in the
bath too. Weave ribbons
through the tops of the
baskets for a finishing touch,
then fill with soaps, rolled
washcloths and some rubber
duckies just for fun.

Broiled Parmesan Tomatoes

Debi DeVore
Dover, OH

A delicious garnish for summer meals.

3 tomatoes, halved
1 T. olive oil
1 clove garlic, minced
1/4 t. pepper

1 T. fresh basil, minced
3/4 c. soft bread crumbs
2 T. grated Parmesan cheese

Arrange tomato halves cut-side up on a broiler pan sprayed with non-stick vegetable spray; set aside. Combine oil, garlic and pepper; brush over tomatoes and sprinkle with basil. Broil about 6 inches from heat for 3 to 4 minutes, until heated through. In a small bowl, combine bread crumbs and Parmesan cheese; sprinkle over tomatoes. Broil an additional one to 2 minutes, until crumbs are golden. Serve immediately. Makes 6 servings.

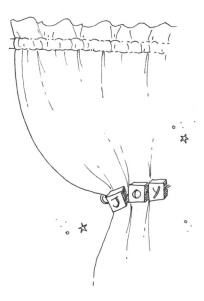

Clever curtain tie-backs...drill holes through small wooden alphabet blocks, then string them together on cord. Spell out light-hearted words like JOY or LOVE.

Sweet Onion Casserole

Jacqueline Kurtz
Reading, PA

A creamy, satisfying bake for onion lovers.

4 sweet onions, quartered
7 T. butter, divided
3 eggs
5-oz. can evaporated milk
1 sleeve round buttery crackers,
    crushed and divided

1-1/2 c. shredded Cheddar
    cheese
salt and pepper to taste

Cover onions with water in a saucepan; boil until tender. Drain.
Melt 4 tablespoons butter in a skillet over medium heat; sauté onions
until golden. Beat eggs and milk together; add sautéed onions, half
of cracker crumbs, cheese, salt and pepper. Spoon into a greased
13"x9" baking pan and bake at 375 degrees for 35 minutes. Melt
remaining butter and stir in remaining cracker crumbs. Top onions
with crumb mixture; bake an additional 15 minutes. Serves 8 to 10.

Take up knitting....even beginners can turn out warm, colorful
scarves or throws. Take a short class, head to the
yarn shop for yarns in glorious colors and textures
and get knitting!

Fresh & Tasty

Cajun Oven Fries

Kathy McLaren
Visalia, CA

Hot and spicy...why settle for ordinary fries?

3 to 4 T. olive oil
2 T. hot pepper sauce
1 t. dried thyme
1 t. ground cumin

1 t. paprika
4 potatoes, cut into wedges
salt and pepper to taste

Combine oil, pepper sauce and seasonings in a large bowl; toss with potatoes. Arrange potatoes in a single layer on an ungreased non-stick baking sheet. Sprinkle to taste with salt and pepper. Bake at 450 degrees for 20 minutes, turning once, until tender. Serves 4.

Add some fun to plain window shades...simply use fabric glue to attach trim along the edge.

Minnesota Carrot-Asparagus Bake

Mary Scurti
Highland, CA

This recipe is a tradition at our holiday table.

1-1/2 c. carrots, peeled and
   chopped
1 c. onion, sliced
3 T. butter
3 T. all-purpose flour
1-1/2 c. milk
16-oz. jar pasteurized process
   cheese sauce

1 t. salt
1 t. pepper
10-oz. pkg. frozen asparagus,
   thawed and drained
2.8-oz. can French fried onions

Combine carrots and onion in a saucepan. Cover with water and
boil until almost tender; drain. Set aside. Mix butter, flour, milk and
cheese sauce; add salt and pepper. Set aside. Layer carrot mixture with
asparagus in a greased 9"x9" baking pan; stir in cheese mixture.
Top with onions; bake at 350 degrees for 15 to 20 minutes, or until
heated through. Serves 8.

Pick up a dozen pint Mason jars...perfect for serving cold
beverages at informal gatherings.

Fresh & Tasty

Cheesy Broccoli-Rice Casserole

Darla Manninen
South Range, MI

I'm always asked to bring this yummy casserole along to family gatherings. Once you taste it, you'll see why!

10-oz. pkg. frozen chopped
  broccoli, thawed
1 c. instant rice, uncooked
1 c. water
10-3/4 oz. can cream of
  celery soup

8-oz. jar pasteurized process
  cheese sauce
1/4 c. margarine, melted
1/2 c. celery, diced
1/2 c. onion, chopped

Mix all ingredients together; spoon into a lightly greased 2-quart casserole dish. Bake at 350 degrees for 1-1/4 hours, stirring every 20 minutes. Serves 4 to 6.

Merry musical placemats! Have photocopies made of vintage sheet music. Sprinkle with glitter, stars or spangles before covering with clear adhesive plastic. Festive!

Scalloped Corn

Neta Liebscher
El Reno, OK

Everyone knows the best home-cooked food is found at church fellowship dinners! This is a favorite of mine.

16-oz. can creamed corn
1/2 c. cracker crumbs
2 eggs, beaten
1/4 c. butter, melted
1/4 c. milk
1/4 c. carrots, peeled
    and shredded

1/4 c. celery, chopped
2 T. green pepper, chopped
2 T. onion, chopped
1 t. salt
1/2 t. sugar
1/2 c. shredded Cheddar cheese

Combine all ingredients except cheese and pour into a lightly greased 2-quart casserole dish. Sprinkle with cheese; bake at 350 degrees for 22 to 30 minutes. Serves 8 to 10.

Are the fridge doors overwhelmed with children's crayon masterpieces? Select a few special drawings to have matted and framed...the kids will be so proud!

Eleanor's Macaroni & Cheese

Carrie Wagner
Stow, OH

Why settle for boxed mac & cheese when this recipe is so easy?

16-oz. container cottage cheese
8-oz. container sour cream
1 egg, beaten
3/4 t. salt
1/2 t. pepper

8-oz. pkg. shredded sharp
    Cheddar cheese
8-oz. pkg. elbow macaroni,
    cooked
Garnish: paprika

Stir together all ingredients except macaroni and paprika in a large bowl. Mix well; stir in macaroni. Spoon mixture into a lightly greased 2-quart casserole dish; sprinkle with paprika. Bake at 350 degrees for 45 minutes; let stand 10 to 15 minutes before serving. Serves 6 to 8.

Work a little decorating magic on plain lampshades with spray paint and fringe, ribbon or trim. Hot glue a whimsical object to the top as a new finial...large beads, tiny figures or pretty seashells are all good choices.

Loaded Baked Potato Casserole

Shannon Franklin
Hartsville, SC

In a word...scrumptious!

3 lbs. potatoes, peeled,
   cubed and boiled
16-oz. container sour cream
1/2 c. butter, melted
8-oz. pkg. shredded sharp
   Cheddar cheese

5 slices bacon, crisply cooked
   and crumbled
Optional: shredded sharp
   Cheddar cheese

Mash together potatoes, sour cream and butter. Put mixture into a
lightly greased 13"x9" baking pan; top with cheese and bacon.
Mix well. Top with additional cheese if desired; bake at 350 degrees
for 15 minutes, or heated through and cheese is melted. Serves 6 to 8.

Patterned china plates all hung in a row are a nostalgic
kitchen accent. Hang them up in a twinkling with plate hangers
from the hardware store.

Green Beans with Bacon & Garlic

Diane Stout
Zeeland, MI

*I invented this recipe so my daughter would enjoy eating green beans.
It's good made with either fresh or frozen beans.*

6 slices bacon
1/4 c. butter
2 t. garlic, minced

salt and pepper to taste
1 lb. green beans, cut into
     bite-size pieces and cooked

Cook bacon in a skillet over medium heat until crisp; drain and crumble bacon. Add butter, garlic, salt and pepper to skillet; continue cooking until butter is melted. Place beans in a serving bowl; toss with bacon mixture and serve immediately. Makes 4 servings.

Craft supplies and toys are easily rounded up in big
baskets...turn clutter into charm.

Tomatoes Provençale

Caroline Capper
Circleville, OH

The mingled flavors of bacon, garlic, onion and mushrooms are wonderful with fresh, ripe tomatoes straight from the garden.

4 slices bacon, diced
1 clove garlic, minced
1 onion, sliced
1/4 lb. sliced mushrooms
1 T. all-purpose flour

1/4 t. seasoned salt
5 tomatoes, sliced
6 T. grated Parmesan cheese, divided
1 T. butter, diced

Cook bacon in a skillet over medium heat until crisp; remove bacon to a paper towel and reserve drippings in skillet. Add garlic, onion and mushrooms to skillet; sauté until tender. Stir in bacon, flour and seasoned salt; set aside. Arrange half of tomato slices in a lightly greased 8"x8" baking pan; spoon half of bacon mixture over top. Sprinkle with 3 tablespoons Parmesan cheese; repeat layers. Dot with butter; bake at 350 degrees for 25 minutes. Serves 6.

The easiest way ever to give country charm to a kitchen windowsill...fill a variety of bottles with colored water and line 'em up on the sill. Sunlight shining through the water will sparkle all day long.

Fresh & Tasty

Mom's Fried Yellow Wax Beans

June Clark
Montrose, MI

*My mom fixed these beans for years, fresh from the garden.
I can never seem to have enough of these on the table
for my family and guests!*

2 T. margarine	2 c. water
2 lbs. yellow wax beans,	3/4 c. milk
cut into bite-size pieces	1 t. salt
3/4 t. baking soda	1/4 t. pepper

Melt margarine in a skillet over medium heat; add beans and sauté until golden. Add baking soda and water; simmer until tender, adding more water if necessary. Stir in milk, salt and pepper; heat through. Serves 8 to 10.

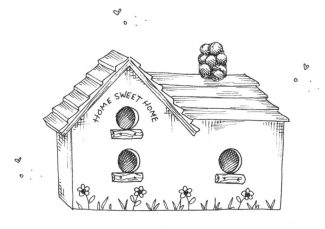

Be it ever so humble, there's no place like home.

−J. Howard Payne

Mushroom & Barley Casserole
Anne Marie Verdiramo
Rochester, MN

*My large family loves this recipe! It has even
been published in my grandmother's church cookbook.*

3/4 c. quick-cooking barley,
   uncooked
1/2 c. onion, chopped
1/4 c. butter

4-oz. can sliced mushrooms
14-1/2 oz. can chicken broth
1/2 c. sliced almonds

Sauté barley and onion in butter until golden; spoon into a greased
1-1/2 quart casserole dish. Add mushrooms with their liquid and
chicken broth; mix well. Bake, covered, at 350 degrees for
1-1/4 hours; sprinkle with almonds. Bake for an additional
15 minutes. Serves 4 to 6.

It's extra-easy to give walls a new look with a sponge-painted
finish. Simply take a natural sponge, dip it lightly into a plate of
latex paint and blot against a paper towel. Press sponge lightly
onto wall and repeat until wall is covered.

Fresh & Tasty

Quick Rice & Black Beans

Erin Tingle
Ephrata, PA

This simple, foolproof recipe goes very well with Mexican chicken.

1 T. olive oil
1 green pepper, chopped
1 onion, chopped
2 cloves garlic, minced
1 c. long-cooking rice, uncooked

16-oz. can black beans,
   drained and rinsed
16-oz. jar salsa
1 c. water

Heat oil in a large skillet over medium heat. Sauté pepper, onion and garlic for about 5 minutes, or until onion is translucent. Add rice, stirring to coat with oil. Add beans, salsa and water, stirring to mix. Cover and simmer over medium-low heat for 20 minutes, stirring once or twice, until rice is tender. Serves 4 to 6.

The easiest-ever holder for useful kitchen string...simply invert a pretty flowerpot over it and pull string right through the hole in the bottom of the pot.

Baked Swiss Potatoes

SueMary Burford-Smith
Tulsa, OK

A delicious change from Cheddar cheesy potatoes.

6 potatoes, peeled, sliced
   and divided
salt and pepper to taste
1-1/2 c. shredded Swiss cheese,
   divided

1/4 t. nutmeg
2 T. butter, diced
10-1/2 oz. can beef broth

Spread one-third of potato slices in a greased 2-quart casserole dish.
Sprinkle with salt, pepper and one-third of cheese. Repeat layers twice,
ending with cheese. Sprinkle with nutmeg, dot with butter and pour
broth over all. Bake, uncovered, at 375 degrees for one hour, until
golden and bubbly. Serves 6 to 8.

Give thrift-shop frames a new look...glue on small items like
buttons, bottle caps, beads or tiny shells. Use one kind of item to
cover the whole frame or mix & match for variety.

Fresh & Tasty

Country Tomato & Onion Bake

Bonnie Weber
West Palm Beach, FL

I always get rave reviews when I serve this at summer cookouts!

4 sweet onions, thinly sliced
   and divided
4 tomatoes, sliced and divided
1 t. salt, divided
1/4 t. pepper, divided

1/2 t. dried basil, divided
1-1/2 c. shredded Cheddar
   cheese, divided
1/2 c. bread crumbs
3 T. butter, melted

In a saucepan over medium heat, simmer onions in boiling water for
10 minutes. Drain and set aside. Arrange half the tomatoes in a
greased 1-1/2 quart casserole dish; top with half the onions. Sprinkle
with half the seasonings and half the cheese; repeat layers. Set aside.
Toss bread crumbs with butter; sprinkle over cheese. Bake at
350 degrees for 30 to 35 minutes, or until tomatoes are tender.
Serves 6.

An old wooden chair that's
lost its seat can find
whimsical new life in the
garden...simply pop a large
flower planter into
the seat opening.

Cavatelli Pasta & Broccoli

Christine Esposito
Saddle Brook, NJ

If you can't find cavatelli, medium shells can be substituted.

2 cloves garlic, chopped
2 T. olive oil
2 10-oz. pkgs. frozen
   chopped broccoli, thawed
2 c. chicken broth

1 T. all-purpose flour
2 T. butter, melted
16-oz. pkg. cavatelli pasta,
   cooked

In a saucepan over medium heat, sauté garlic in oil until tender.
Add broccoli and sauté for one minute; pour in chicken broth.
Simmer for 3 minutes; set aside. In a separate saucepan, combine
flour and butter; heat on low setting until thickened. Stir into broccoli
mixture, cooking until dissolved; pour over prepared pasta.
Serves 6 to 8.

*Oh-so-easy iced tea...fill up a 2-quart pitcher with water and
drop in 6 to 8 teabags. Refrigerate overnight. Discard teabags
and add ice cubes and sugar to taste...cool and refreshing!*

Copper Penny Carrots

*Beverly Mock
Pensacola, FL*

Kids love these carrots!

2 lbs. carrots, peeled,
   sliced and cooked
1 onion, sliced
1 green pepper, sliced
10-3/4 oz. can tomato soup
1 c. sugar

3/4 c. vinegar
1/2 c. corn oil
1/2 t. dry mustard
1 t. Worcestershire sauce
salt and pepper to taste

Layer carrots, onion and pepper in a lightly greased 13"x9" baking pan; set aside. Combine remaining ingredients; pour over carrot mixture. Refrigerate overnight. Serves 8 to 10.

A little old wooden baby swing makes a sweet hanger for a potted plant in the corner of a porch. Add a fresh coat of paint or simply leave it as-is for rustic charm.

Creamy Spinach Casserole

Mary Lynn Rabon
Mobile, AL

Even picky eaters will love this oh-so-easy spinach dish!

2 10-oz. pkgs. frozen
   chopped spinach
8-oz. pkg. cream cheese, cubed
10-3/4 oz. can cream of
   mushroom soup

6-oz. can French fried
   onions, divided

Cook spinach according to package directions. Drain; place in an ungreased one-quart casserole dish. Blend in cream cheese until melted; add mushroom soup and half of onions. Top with remaining onions. Bake at 350 degrees for 30 minutes, until hot and bubbly. Serves 4 to 6.

An old-fashioned wicker bicycle basket makes a unique wall pocket in the kitchen.

Warm & Comforting

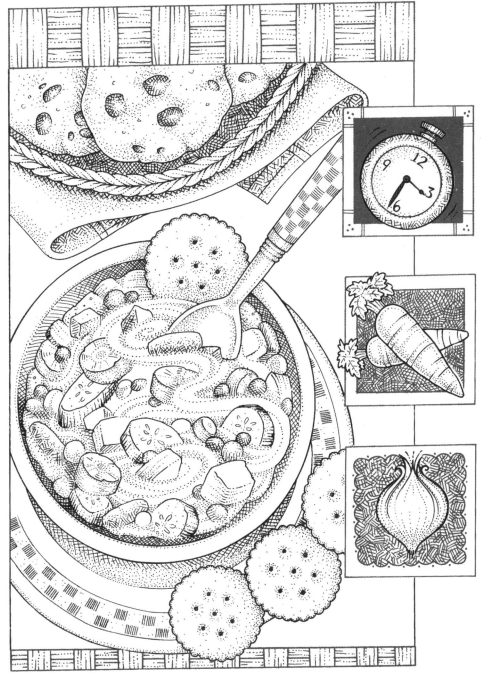

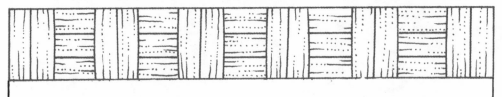

Cheddar-Ham Chowder

Sue Roberson
Peoria, AZ

Stamp the snow off your boots and enjoy a cup of this rich, creamy soup...it will warm you up on winter day.

2 c. potatoes, peeled and cubed
1/2 c. carrots, peeled and sliced
1/2 c. celery, sliced
1/4 c. onion, chopped
2 c. water
1 t. salt
1/4 t. pepper

1/4 c. butter
1/4 c. all-purpose flour
2 c. milk
8-oz. pkg. shredded Cheddar
    cheese
15-oz. can corn, drained
1-1/2 c. cooked ham, cubed

In a saucepan, bring potatoes, carrots, celery, onion, water, salt and pepper to a boil. Reduce heat; simmer for 8 to 10 minutes, or until vegetables are tender. Remove from heat; set aside. Melt butter in another saucepan over low heat; blend in flour. Pour in milk; cook and stir until thickened. Sprinkle in cheese and stir until melted; stir into potato mixture. Return to low heat; add corn and ham. Cook until heated through. Makes 6 to 8 servings.

A soup supper is warm and comforting on a cold night...so easy too! Add a loaf of bread and a fruit cobbler for dessert...done!

warm & Comforting

Cheesy Broccoli-Potato Soup

Darlene Luker
Grapeland, TX

This soup is wonderful on a cold day and even better reheated the next day.

7 potatoes, peeled and cubed
10-oz. pkg. frozen chopped
  broccoli, thawed
10-3/4 oz. can cream of
  mushroom soup
10-3/4 oz. can cream of
  celery soup

10-3/4 oz. can cream of
  chicken soup
16-oz. pkg. pasteurized process
  cheese spread
salt, pepper and garlic powder
  to taste

Combine potatoes and broccoli in a saucepan; cover with water. Bring to a boil over medium heat; cook until potatoes are tender. Drain and add remaining ingredients. Cook until heated through. Serves 8 to 10.

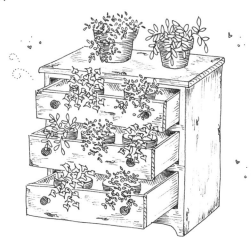

Turn an old dresser into a garden! Set on a sunny porch, then pull out the drawers slightly, line with plastic and nestle potted plants inside to trail down the front. Set more pots of flowers on top.

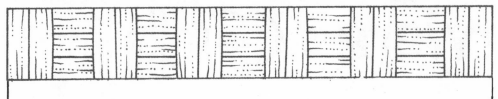

Shells & Chicken Soup

Kimberley Moran
Glendale, AZ

Broccoli and tomatoes add color to this flavorful chicken soup.

3 boneless, skinless chicken
    breasts, cubed
1/2 t. dried basil
1/8 t. red pepper flakes
salt and pepper to taste

1-1/2 c. broccoli, chopped
14-1/2 oz. can diced tomatoes
2 10-1/2 oz. cans chicken broth
8-oz. pkg. small shell macaroni,
    cooked

In a large skillet sprayed with non-stick vegetable spray, cook chicken over medium heat until no longer pink; sprinkle with seasonings. Add broccoli; cook for 4 to 5 minutes. Stir in tomatoes; simmer for 3 to 4 minutes. Add broth and shells; simmer for an additional 15 to 20 minutes. Serves 4 to 6.

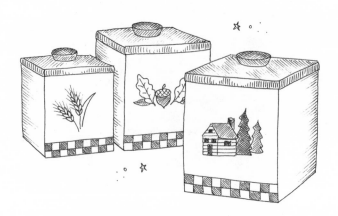

Need to thicken a kettle of soup? Just stir in a
little quick-cooking oatmeal.

No-Peek Stew

Phyllis Peters
Three Rivers, MI

My Aunt Mary shared this recipe with me years ago.
Pop it in the oven and you're free to shop, garden or visit
with friends, knowing dinner will be ready right on time.

1 lb. stew beef, cubed
4 potatoes, peeled and cubed
4 carrots, peeled and chopped
4 stalks celery, chopped
3 onions, chopped

2 c. stewed tomatoes
14-1/2 oz. can beef broth
5 T. tapioca, uncooked
1 t. salt
pepper to taste

Combine all ingredients in a greased 13"x9" baking pan; cover.
Bake at 325 degrees for 4 hours. Serves 8.

Make an oh-so-simple gallery for school photos, vacation
snapshots and other favorite photos! Attach a length of wooden
trim molding to the wall, then tack on some clip clothespins along
the molding and clip on your photos.

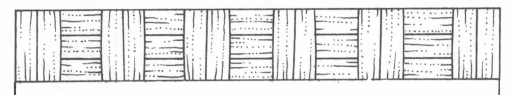

Zesty Barley Stew

Cyndy Rogers
Upton, MA

This recipe is very satisfying and fills the kitchen with a wonderful aroma. I like to double it and enjoy leftovers for lunch the next day.

3 carrots, peeled and sliced
3 stalks celery, sliced
1 onion, chopped
4 c. water
1/2 c. long-cooking barley,
   uncooked

1-1/2 oz. pkg. savory herb
   with garlic soup mix
17-oz. can corn, drained
15-oz. can white beans,
   drained and rinsed

In a stockpot sprayed with non-stick vegetable spray, cook carrots, celery and onion over medium heat for 3 minutes. Stir in water, barley and soup mix. Bring to a boil; reduce heat. Simmer for 30 minutes, until barley is tender. Mix in corn and beans; simmer for an additional 5 minutes, until heated through. Serves 6.

A pitcher of cool water is a thoughtful touch on the guest room nightstand. No carafe? Simply fill a tall glass with water, then invert a short fat tumbler over it. Drop in a slice of lemon for eye appeal.

Spicy Taco Soup

Carolyn Curry
Hale Center, TX

*This recipe makes a big pot of soup that's great served
with cornbread or fresh tortillas. For a spicier soup,
use the whole package of taco seasoning.*

1-1/2 lbs. ground beef
1 onion, chopped
1 green pepper, chopped
2 14-1/2 oz. cans diced
   tomatoes
14-1/2 oz. can tomatoes
   with chiles
16-oz. can pinto beans
   with jalapeños

16-oz. can pinto beans
16-oz. can white hominy
16-oz. can yellow hominy
1-1/2 T. taco seasoning mix
1-oz. pkg. ranch salad
   dressing mix
Garnish: shredded Mexican-
   blend cheese

In a soup pot over medium heat, brown ground beef with onion and
pepper. Drain; add remaining ingredients except cheese. Reduce heat
and simmer for 30 to 45 minutes, until hot and bubbly. Garnish with
shredded cheese. Serves 12 to 15.

Grow a windowsill garden...fun
for kids! Fill an empty jar with
water, then use toothpicks to
suspend the leafy top of a carrot
or pineapple. An avocado pit works
well too. Set in a sunny window.
The new plant will form roots and
leaves in only a few days.

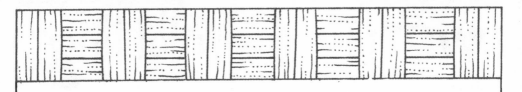

Pumpkin Soup with Curry

Jodi Civill
Ravena, NY

A delightfully different starter for autumn meals.

1/2 c. onion, chopped	15-oz. can pumpkin
2 T. butter	12-oz. can evaporated milk
2 T. all-purpose flour	1 T. honey
1 t. curry powder	1/2 t. nutmeg
3 c. chicken broth	salt and pepper to taste

In a large saucepan over medium heat, cook onion in butter until softened. Add flour and curry powder; cook and stir for about 2 minutes. Whisk in broth. Bring to a boil; add remaining ingredients. Simmer until heated through, about 20 to 30 minutes. Serves 6.

It's easy to make a jar of crystallized honey useable again. Set it in a small saucepan of simmering water...the crystals will dissolve after several minutes.

warm & Comforting

Mashed Potato Soup

Mike Davis
Port Orchard, WA

Cheesy and comforting.

4 potatoes, peeled and chopped
4 c. water
2 cloves garlic, minced
2 cubes chicken bouillon

1 c. pasteurized process cheese
  spread, cubed
1 to 1-1/2 c. half-and-half

Boil potatoes in water over medium heat until soft and soupy; add garlic and bouillon. Reduce heat; stir until potatoes are nearly mashed. Add cheese; stir until melted. Add one cup half-and-half; simmer for 5 minutes. Add remaining half-and-half to thin, if desired. Serves 4.

Check the pantry and fridge for garnishes that will dress up a plain salad in a jiffy! Chopped nuts, crushed corn chips, minced fresh herbs, sliced olives and even the crumbled bacon left from breakfast can all add flavor and color.

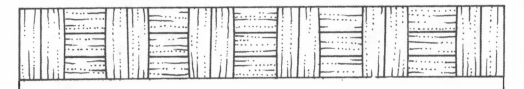

Tailgate Seafood Chowder

Kathleen Brillinger
Norwich, NY

So easy to make, your guests will think you worked for hours!

1 lb. shrimp, peeled, cleaned and chopped
1/2 c. butter
3 8-oz. cans chopped clams, drained
2 10-1/2 oz. cans she-crab soup
2 19-oz. cans chunky clam chowder
1/2 c. vermouth or chicken broth
pepper to taste
Garnish: fresh parsley, chopped

Sauté shrimp in butter over medium heat in a large saucepan. When shrimp turn pink, add remaining ingredients except parsley; heat through. Sprinkle with parsley. Serves 8 to 10.

Give old candles new glow! Grate partially burned candles with a kitchen grater, then layer clear glass jars with wax shavings in different colors. Push a wick down into the center and enjoy the candles a second time.

warm & Comforting

Shrimp Bisque

Jennie Parker
Rochester, NY

*Garnish with a dollop of unsweetened whipped cream
for an extra-special presentation.*

1 c. potatoes, peeled and diced
1 c. celery, chopped
1/2 c. onion, chopped
1 c. water
1/2 t. salt
1/8 t. pepper

2 c. milk
3 T. all-purpose flour
2 4-1/2 oz. cans tiny shrimp,
    drained
2 T. butter
Garnish: fresh parsley, snipped

In a saucepan over medium heat, combine potatoes, celery, onion, water, salt and pepper. Cover and simmer for 15 minutes, or until potatoes are tender. Whisk together milk and flour in a bowl until smooth; stir into mixture along with shrimp and butter. Cook and stir over low heat until thick and bubbly. Garnish with parsley. Makes 4 servings.

Why not get out Mom's soup tureen set for cozy soup dinners
with your family? The ladle makes serving easy and the lid
keeps soup piping hot and steamy...perfect!

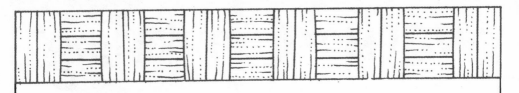

Creamy Artichoke Soup

Sarah Davis
Gig Harbor, WA

We love this served with crusty French bread and sweet butter.

1/2 c. green onion, chopped
2 carrots, peeled and sliced
2 stalks celery, chopped
1/2 c. butter, softened and
   divided
4 c. chicken broth
14-oz. can artichokes, chopped

1-1/2 c. sliced mushrooms
1/2 t. dried thyme
1/2 t. dried oregano
1 bay leaf
3 T. all-purpose flour
1 c. whipping cream

In a large saucepan, sauté onion, carrots and celery in 1/4 cup butter. Add broth, artichokes, mushrooms and herbs. Bring to a simmer for 20 minutes. In a bowl, combine remaining butter, flour and cream; stir into soup. Simmer for an additional 10 minutes. Discard bay leaf before serving. Serves 10.

Mix up some fragrant potpourri. Pare orange or lemon peels into thin strips and toss with a little cinnamon or allspice. Add some whole cloves and set in a pretty bowl to dry.

Chicken Soup Au Gratin

Casii Dodd
Frederick, MD

So much flavor...so little effort!

2 boneless, skinless chicken
  breasts
2 c. water
1/2 t. salt
1/2 c. onion, chopped
1/2 c. carrots, peeled and
  chopped

1/2 c. celery, chopped
10-3/4 oz. can cream of
  chicken soup
1/2 c. milk
1/8 t. pepper
1 c. shredded Cheddar cheese

Combine chicken, water and salt in a saucepan over medium heat;
simmer until tender. Remove chicken, reserving broth in saucepan;
let cool, then dice and set aside. Add vegetables to broth in pan;
simmer until tender. Stir in soup, milk and pepper; add cheese and
chicken. Heat through, stirring until cheese melts. Serves 4 to 6.

Home...that blessed word, which opens to the
human heart the most perfect glimpse of Heaven.
–Lydia M. Child

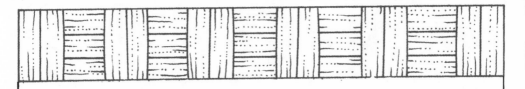

Hearty Cheeseburger Soup

Julie Howard
Jacksonville, FL

Pick up a package of precooked bacon strips for an easy garnish...snip with kitchen shears and they're ready in a snap.

2 c. potatoes, peeled and cubed
2 carrots, peeled and grated
1 onion, chopped
1 jalapeño, seeded and chopped
1 clove garlic, minced
1-1/2 c. water
1 T. beef bouillon granules
1/2 t. salt
1 lb. ground beef, browned
   and drained

2-1/2 c. milk, divided
3 T. all-purpose flour
8-oz. pkg. American cheese,
   cubed
Optional: 1/4 to 1 t. cayenne
   pepper
1/2 lb. bacon, crisply cooked
   and crumbled

Combine first 8 ingredients in a large saucepan; bring to a boil.
Reduce heat and simmer for 15 to 20 minutes, until potatoes are
tender. Stir in beef and 2 cups milk; cook until heated through.
In a bowl, mix flour and remaining milk until smooth; stir into soup.
Bring to a boil; cook for 2 minutes. Reduce heat; stir in cheese until
melted. Stir in cayenne pepper, if using; sprinkle with bacon.
Serves 6 to 8.

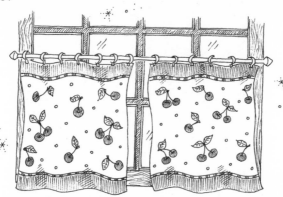

Turn Mom's vintage tea towels into cafe curtains in a
jiffy...simply attach clip-on curtain rings.

Warm & Comforting

Sausage & Wild Rice Chowder

Susan Ruppert
Milligan, NE

Hearty and satisfying...hits the spot after a brisk hike in the woods.

3/4 lb. ground sausage
1 onion, chopped
1/3 c. all-purpose flour
4-1/2 c. water
1/2 c. long-cooking brown rice,
  uncooked

1/2 c. long-cooking wild rice,
  uncooked
1-1/3 c. chicken broth
12-oz. can evaporated milk
1 T. chicken bouillon granules
2-1/2 c. American cheese, grated

Brown sausage and onion over medium heat in a skillet. Drain;
blend in flour and water. Stir in rice and chicken broth; bring to a boil.
Reduce heat to a simmer for 35 to 40 minutes. Add evaporated milk
and bouillon; cook for 8 to 10 minutes, until heated through
and bouillon is dissolved. Sprinkle with cheese. Serves 8.

*Mount a row of big enameled hooks on a peg
board...perfect for keeping mugs handy for a steamy
cup of tea or a helping of soup!*

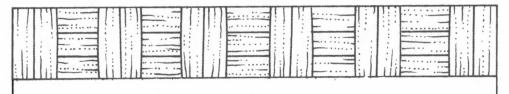

Senate Bean Soup

Kristi Stubbs
Colbert, OK

This soup is easily prepared in a slow cooker...cover and cook
for 6 to 8 hours on low setting. Ready when you are!

2 10-3/4 oz. cans bean
    and bacon soup
15-1/8 oz. can Great Northern
    beans
15-oz. can navy beans
16-oz. can pinto beans
    with jalapeños

1 onion, chopped
1 green pepper, chopped
1-1/2 t. celery seed
1 lb. Polish sausage,
    thinly sliced
1-3/4 c. water

Combine all ingredients in a stockpot. Simmer over low heat for one
hour. Serves 8 to 10.

Create a comfy spot
for reading favorite
books or just
daydreaming...create a
window seat with a
flip-top chest topped
with a cushion. Add a
drift of soft pillows and
stow a cozy throw
inside the chest.

Corn Chowder

Amy Walters
Orem, UT

Make this hearty soup even heartier by stirring in some cooked, chopped chicken breast.

1/4 lb. bacon
1 onion, chopped
4 stalks celery, chopped
8 c. chicken broth, divided
4 redskin potatoes, peeled
   and chopped

1 bay leaf
3 T. all-purpose flour
16-oz. pkg. frozen corn
1/2 to 1 c. whipping cream
salt and pepper to taste

Cook bacon in a stockpot over medium heat until crisp. Set aside, leaving drippings in pot. Sauté onion and celery in drippings until tender. Add 7 cups chicken broth, potatoes and bay leaf. Boil until potatoes are tender, about 10 minutes. Combine remaining broth and flour in a plastic zipping bag; shake until smooth. Pour into potato mixture; stir in corn, cream, salt and pepper. Cook until heated through; add bacon. Discard bay leaf before serving. Serves 4 to 6.

Homemade chicken broth is delicious and easy with a slow cooker. Combine 6 chicken thighs with some chopped carrots, celery and onion. Top with 6 cups water, cover and cook on low setting for 8 to 10 hours. Strain broth, refrigerate and skim fat. The cooked chicken is delicious in soups and salads.

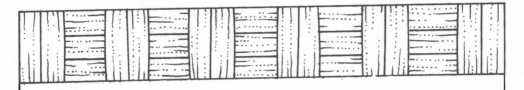

French Onion Soup

Barbara Feist Stienstra
Goshen, NY

The flavor of this soup is divine! The recipe was created
at the college where I worked for many years.

1 t. butter
2 t. olive oil
4 onions, sliced
3 c. beef broth

3 to 4 bay leaves
salt and pepper to taste
6 slices French bread
3/4 c. shredded Swiss cheese

Heat butter and oil together in a stockpot until butter melts. Add onions; cook over medium heat for 20 to 30 minutes, until dark golden. Add broth, bay leaves, salt and pepper. Bring to a boil; reduce heat, cover and simmer for 30 minutes. Remove and discard bay leaves; set aside. Arrange bread on an ungreased broiler pan; sprinkle with cheese and broil until golden. Divide soup among 6 soup bowls; top each with a slice of toasted bread. Serves 6.

Make everyday grilled cheese sandwiches
special...grill 'em in a waffle iron!

Chicken-Tortellini Soup

Chris McCain
Mosinee, WI

Quick, easy and delicious.

1 lb. boneless, skinless chicken
    breast, cooked and cubed
9-oz. pkg. cheese tortellini,
    uncooked
46-oz. can chicken broth
1 c. carrots, peeled and chopped

1/2 c. onion, chopped
1/2 c. celery, sliced
1/2 t. dried thyme
1/4 t. pepper
1 bay leaf

Combine all ingredients in a stockpot; bring to a boil over medium heat. Reduce heat, cover and simmer until tortellini is tender. Discard bay leaf. Serves 6.

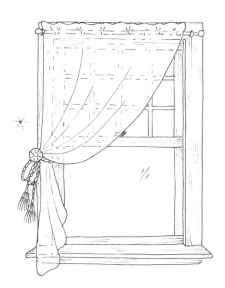

Sparkly glass door knobs make creative curtain tie-backs...simply mount on each side of a window, then pull a tasseled cord back over the knobs.

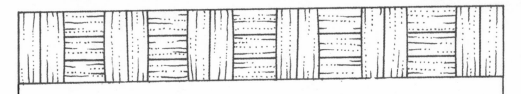

Hot Pepper Stew

Yuma Carter
Milroy, IN

*My family always enjoyed this stew at a local restaurant.
When the restaurant went out of business, I adapted recipes
until I had one that I think is equally good.*

2 c. beef chuck roast,
  cooked and shredded
2 16-oz. cans butter beans,
  drained and rinsed
14-oz. can beef broth

14-1/2 oz. can diced tomatoes
  with peppers and onions
10-oz. can tomatoes with chiles
Optional: diced green chiles
  to taste

Place all ingredients in a stockpot; cook over medium heat until
mixture boils. Reduce heat and simmer for 1-1/2 hours. Serves 6 to 8.

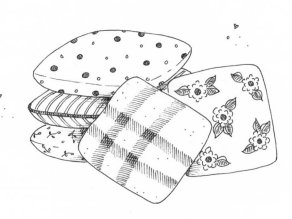

Stock up on plump, oversized pillows
for extra seating when guests are visiting...it's easy to keep
'em stashed away under a coffee table.

Colby-Swiss Broccoli Soup

Johnda Tompkins
Rushville, IN

This cheesy soup will warm you up in a jiffy!

1/2 c. water
1-1/2 t. chicken bouillon
   granules
4 c. broccoli flowerets
1 c. carrots, peeled and sliced
3 T. butter
1/4 c. green onion, sliced

3 T. all-purpose flour
1/4 to 1/2 t. nutmeg
1/4 t. pepper
3 c. milk
2 c. shredded Colby cheese
1 c. shredded Swiss cheese

Combine water and bouillon in a 3-quart saucepan; bring to a boil. Add broccoli and carrots; return to a boil. Reduce heat; cover and cook for about 10 minutes, until vegetables are tender. Drain, reserving liquid. Set aside. Melt butter; add onion and cook until tender. Stir in flour, nutmeg and pepper. Cook for one minute; gradually add milk and reserved liquid. Heat until thickened; sprinkle in cheeses. Stir until cheeses are melted; add broccoli and carrots. Serves 6.

Curl up on the sofa with your family to watch a favorite movie...what could be cozier on a chilly night?

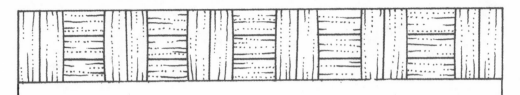

Risi Bisi

Karen Pilcher
Burleson, TX

This Italian rice and pea soup is so filling and comforting in the wintertime! It will become quite thick as it cools, so add a little water or chicken broth when reheating.

3 T. onion, chopped
1/4 c. plus 2 T. butter
10-oz. pkg. frozen peas
1/2 t. salt

6 c. chicken broth
1 c. long-cooking rice, uncooked
3 T. fresh parsley, chopped
2/3 c. grated Parmesan cheese

Sauté onion in butter in a large saucepan until tender. Add peas and salt; cook for 2 minutes, stirring often. Add broth and bring to a boil; stir in rice. Reduce to low heat and simmer for 25 minutes, or until rice is tender. Stir in parsley and remove from heat; sprinkle with cheese at serving time. Serves 4 to 6.

Take the kids to a paint-your-own pottery shop! Let them decorate cheery soup bowls for the whole family. Their creations will warm hearts and tummies at the same time.

warm & Comforting

Slow-Cooker White Chili

Wendy West Hickey
Pittsburgh, PA

*Speed up this recipe by substituting canned beans...you'll
need about three, 15-ounce cans. No soaking required!*

16-oz. pkg. dried Great Northern
  beans
2 lbs. boneless, skinless chicken
  breasts, cubed
14-1/2 oz. can chicken broth
1 c. water
1 onion, chopped

3 cloves garlic, minced
2 4-oz. cans chopped green
  chiles
2 t. ground cumin
1-1/2 t. cayenne pepper
1 t. dried oregano
1/2 t. salt

Soak beans in water overnight; drain. Combine all ingredients in
a slow cooker and stir. Cover and cook on low setting for 10 to
12 hours, or on high setting for 5 to 6 hours, stirring occasionally.
Serves 6 to 8.

Every sofa should have an inviting throw folded over the back
for snuggling! Why not pull out that afghan that Great-Aunt
Sophie crocheted years ago, or a treasured baby quilt that's
been outgrown?

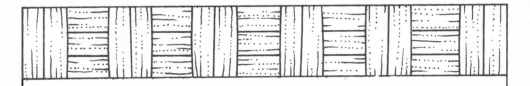

Romano Cheese Bread

Jo Ann

This delicious bread couldn't be easier to make.

1 c. milk	6 eggs, beaten
2 envs. active dry yeast	1-1/2 c. grated Romano cheese
2-1/2 c. all-purpose flour	1 T. butter, softened

Warm milk over low heat to 110 degrees on a cooking thermometer; remove from heat. Add yeast; let stand for 10 minutes, until dissolved. In a large bowl, combine yeast mixture and remaining ingredients; beat well. Divide dough between 2 greased 9"x5" loaf pans. Cover and let rise for 30 minutes, or until nearly double in bulk. Bake at 350 degrees for one hour, until loaves are golden and sound hollow when tapped on the bottom. Remove to wire racks to cool. Makes 2 loaves.

Welcome a new neighbor the country way...pile fresh muffins high in a homespun-lined basket, then tuck in a jar of fruit preserves or clover honey.

Nanny's Cheese Scones

Jennifer Niemi
Nova Scotia, Canada

*When I was a baby, my grandmother came from Scotland to care
for me. Often she would bake cheese scones because, as my mum
says, Nanny just felt like making something nice for us that day!
I still enjoy serving these with vegetable soup.*

1-2/3 c. all-purpose flour
4 t. baking powder
1/4 t. salt
1/2 t. pepper

2 T. butter
1 c. shredded Cheddar cheese
3/4 c. plus 2 T. milk, divided

Sift together flour, baking powder, salt and pepper; cut in butter until
mixture resembles coarse crumbs. Stir in cheese; add 3/4 cup milk and
mix well. On a floured surface, press dough into an 8"x6" rectangle,
one-inch thick. Cut into twelve, 2"x2" squares; place on a greased
baking sheet. Brush tops with remaining milk; bake at 425 degrees for
12 to 15 minutes. Makes one dozen.

Paper collectibles like vacation postcards and birthday cards are
fun to frame. Match them with creative mats like tea towels or
scrapbooking paper. If you prefer, preserve the originals by
framing color photocopies.

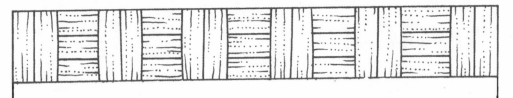

Coconut Bread

Teri Naquin
Melville, LA

Perfect with a tropical fruit salad.

1/2 c. butter, softened	1 c. sweetened flaked coconut
1 c. sugar	2 c. all-purpose flour
2 eggs	1 t. baking powder
2 t. coconut extract	1 t. baking soda
1 c. sour cream	

Blend together butter and sugar in a mixing bowl; beat in eggs and extract. Stir in sour cream; add coconut. Mix well; set aside. In another bowl, combine flour, baking powder and baking soda; stir into butter mixture. Spoon into a greased 9"x5" loaf pan; bake at 350 degrees for 45 to 50 minutes. Makes one loaf.

Make a tea cozy from a pair of quilted oval placemats...it's simple! Put 2 placemats right-side together. Stitch from one short side across the top to the other side, leaving the bottom open and ready to pop over a hot teapot.

Warm & Comforting

Zucchini Bread

Michelle Hawkins
Radcliff, KY

My son, Matthew, loves this zucchini bread!

4 eggs
2 c. sugar
1 c. applesauce
2 t. oil
2 t. water
2 c. zucchini, shredded
3 c. all-purpose flour

2 t. baking soda
1/2 t. baking powder
1-1/2 t. salt
1 t. cinnamon
1 t. vanilla extract
1 c. chopped pecans

Beat eggs, sugar, applesauce, oil and water together in a mixing bowl. Add remaining ingredients and mix well. Pour batter into 2 greased and floured 9"x5" loaf pans. Bake for at 350 degrees for 45 minutes to one hour. Makes 2 loaves.

Re-use a butter dish as a windowsill
planter...simply turn over the lid, set it on the dish and plant with a
tiny, low-growing herb like thyme.

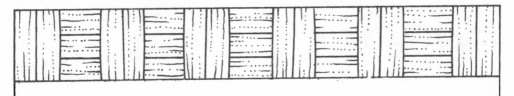

Walnut-Pear Bread

Carol Hickman
Kingsport, TN

A yummy fruit & nut loaf that's out of the ordinary.

1/2 c. oil	1/2 t. salt
1 c. sugar	1/4 t. cinnamon
2 eggs	1/4 t. nutmeg
1/4 c. sour cream	16-oz. can pear halves,
1 t. vanilla extract	drained and mashed
2 c. all-purpose flour	1/2 c. chopped walnuts
1 t. baking soda	

Beat oil and sugar together in a mixing bowl; add eggs. Stir in sour cream and vanilla; add flour, baking soda, salt and spices. Stir in pears and walnuts; pour into a greased 9"x5" loaf pan. Bake at 350 degrees for 45 minutes. Makes one loaf.

Slip sparkly bangle bracelets around rolled dinner napkins for playful table settings!

Banana-Sour Cream Loaf

Virginia Bailey
Seven Hills, OH

This loaf tastes even better if left to stand overnight before cutting...it's delicious toasted too!

2/3 c. butter, softened
1-1/3 c. sugar
2 eggs
1-1/2 c. bananas, mashed
2-3/4 c. all-purpose flour

1 t. baking powder
1 t. baking soda
1/2 t. salt
2/3 c. sour cream
1 c. chopped walnuts

Blend butter and sugar in a mixing bowl until light and fluffy. Add eggs and bananas. Beat until well blended. Sift flour, baking powder, baking soda and salt together in another bowl. Add alternately with sour cream to banana mixture, stirring just to blend. Stir in nuts. Spoon into a 9"x5" loaf pan, greased and floured on bottom only. Bake at 350 degrees for 1-1/4 hours, or until tester comes out clean. Let stand in pan on a wire rack for 20 minutes. Remove from pan and cool; wrap in plastic wrap or aluminum foil. Makes one loaf.

Banana bread is perfect for kids just learning to cook. They'll learn to measure and mix ingredients, and they'll love tasting their creation!

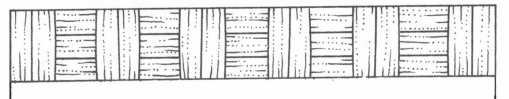

Irish Soda Bread

Michelle Murphy
Madison, CT

Delightful buttered or plain.

3-1/2 c. all-purpose flour	2 T. butter, melted
1/4 c. sugar	1 egg
4 t. baking powder	2 c. buttermilk
1 t. baking soda	8-oz. pkg. raisins
1 t. salt	3 T. caraway seed

Combine flour, sugar, baking powder, baking soda and salt in a mixing bowl. Add butter, egg and buttermilk; stir until well combined. Mix in raisins and caraway seed. Pour into a greased 8" round cake pan or 8"x4" loaf pan. Bake at 325 degrees for 55 minutes to one hour, until top is cracked and golden. Serves 6 to 8.

Wrap up some fragrant potpourri in dainty
embroidered handkerchiefs and tie with gingham ribbon.
Place in a bowl to use as little gifts for visitors.

Hearty Bran Loaf

Janet Frazier
Holland, TX

I like to bake this bread for my grandmama!

2 envs. active dry yeast
1 c. very warm water
3/4 c. sugar
1-1/2 t. salt
2 eggs, beaten

1 c. bran cereal
1 c. boiling water
1/2 c. shortening
6-1/2 c. all-purpose flour

Dissolve yeast in warm water; combine with remaining ingredients in a large bowl and mix well. Divide between 2 greased 9"x5" loaf pans. Bake at 350 degrees for 45 minutes to one hour, until a toothpick inserted in center comes out clean. Makes 2 loaves.

Pair a basket of warm muffins with a crock of fruit butter...yum! Simply blend 1/2 cup each of softened butter and strawberry, apricot or peach preserves.

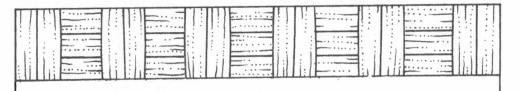

Long-Life Muffins

Barb Kietzer
Niles, MI

Full of stuff that's good and good for you.

2 c. whole-wheat flour
1 T. sugar
1-1/2 t. baking powder
1/2 t. baking soda
1/2 c. tomato sauce
1 t. garlic powder

1/2 c. frozen chopped spinach,
   thawed and drained
1/4 c. olive oil
1 egg
3/4 c. buttermilk
3/4 c. grated Parmesan cheese

Mix flour, sugar, baking powder and baking soda together in a bowl; set aside. Combine remaining ingredients except cheese in another bowl; mix well and stir in cheese. Stir into flour mixture until moistened. Fill 15 paper-lined muffin cups 3/4 full. Bake at 375 degrees for 18 minutes. Makes 15.

Cherish all your happy moments...they make
a fine cushion for old age.
–Booth Tarkington

Sweet Potato Dinner Rolls

*Jennifer Eveland-Kupp
Temple, PA*

Short on time? Use canned sweet potatoes instead.

1 c. sweet potatoes, peeled and
    boiled
3 T. butter, melted
1 env. active dry yeast
1 c. very warm water, divided

1 egg
1 t. salt
3 T. sugar
5 c. all-purpose flour

Mash sweet potatoes with butter; set aside. Dissolve yeast in 1/2 cup warm water; add to potato mixture. Blend in egg, salt and sugar; mix in flour alternately with remaining water. Knead well until smooth and springy, about 2 to 3 minutes. Cover and let rise for 2 hours, until double. Shape into 2-inch balls; arrange on a greased baking sheet. Bake at 425 degrees for 15 to 20 minutes. Makes 1-1/2 to 2 dozen.

Frame a christening outfit in a shadow box, grouped
with a baby photo, a tiny silver rattle and a sweet little
baby spoon. Soft pink or blue fabric is a perfect backdrop
for these sweet reminders of baby days.

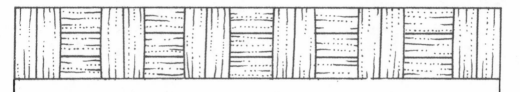

Cheddar-Onion Bread

Susie Backus
Gooseberry Patch

Add a little garlic powder if you like.

1/2 c. onion, finely chopped
2 T. butter
1/2 c. milk
1 egg, beaten

1-1/2 c. biscuit baking mix
1 c. shredded Cheddar cheese,
    divided
2 t. dried parsley

Sauté onion in butter in a small skillet; set aside. Mix together milk, egg and biscuit mix in a mixing bowl; stir in onion, 1/2 cup cheese and parsley. Pour into an 8"x8" baking pan sprayed with non-stick vegetable spray; top with remaining cheese. Bake at 400 degrees for approximately 20 minutes. Serve warm. Serves 8.

Pour olive oil into saucers and sprinkle with a little Italian seasoning...perfect for dipping slices of warm crusty bread.

Amish Biscuits

John Grashoff
Fort Wayne, IN

My grandma's recipe...I like to make these biscuits for our family.

2 c. all-purpose flour
1 T. baking powder
1 t. salt

1/4 c. mayonnaise
1 c. milk
1 t. sugar

Combine flour, baking powder and salt; add remaining ingredients. Drop by tablespoonfuls onto a lightly greased baking sheet. Bake at 375 degrees for 18 to 20 minutes. Makes 2 dozen.

Don't hide that chunky little clay pot or bowl that your child brought home from school! Put it to use as a desktop holder for paperclips and thumb tacks.

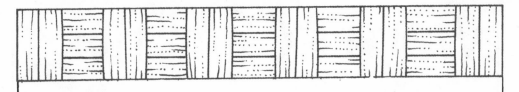

Pumpkin Harvest Bread

Deneen Lotz
Bridgeport, CT

This bread is wonderful with cream cheese!

2 c. sugar
2/3 c. butter, softened
15-oz. can pumpkin
2/3 c. milk
4 eggs, beaten
3-1/3 c. all-purpose flour
2 t. baking soda

1/2 t. baking powder
1-1/2 t. salt
1 t. cinnamon
1 t. ground cloves
2/3 c. raisins
2/3 c. chopped nuts

Blend sugar and butter in a mixing bowl; add pumpkin, milk and eggs. Set aside. Combine flour, baking soda, baking powder, salt and spices in another bowl; stir into pumpkin mixture. Add raisins and nuts. Spoon into 2 greased 8"x4" loaf pans. Bake at 350 degrees for one hour to one hour and 10 minutes, until a toothpick comes out clean. Makes 2 loaves.

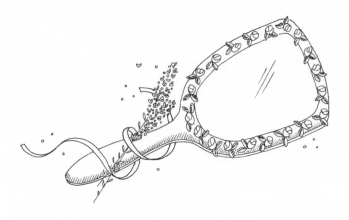

Dress up a plain hand mirror just for fun...simply circle it with tiny silk or ribbon flowers hot glued around the edge.

warm & Comforting

Oatmeal Dinner Rolls

Kris Warner
Circleville, OH

Nothing is more welcoming than the aroma of baking bread!

2 c. cold water
1 c. quick-cooking oats,
    uncooked
3 T. butter
1 env. active dry yeast
1/3 c. very warm water

1/3 c. brown sugar, packed
1 T. sugar
1-1/2 t. salt
4-3/4 to 5-1/4 c. all-purpose
    flour, divided

Bring water to a boil in a saucepan; add oats and butter. Cook and stir for one minute; remove from heat. Cool; set aside. Dissolve yeast in warm water in a large bowl; add oat mixture, sugars, salt and 4 cups flour. Beat until smooth; add enough of remaining flour to form a soft dough. Knead on a floured surface until smooth, about 6 to 8 minutes. Place dough in a greased bowl; cover and let rise until double, about one hour. Punch dough down and let stand for 10 minutes; shape into 18 one-inch balls. Place in 2 greased 9" round cake pans; cover and let rise for 45 minutes. Bake at 350 degrees for 20 to 25 minutes. Remove to wire racks; cool. Makes 1-1/2 dozen.

A pat of homemade garlic butter really adds flavor to warm bread or steamed vegetables. Blend equal parts of softened butter and olive oil, then stir in finely chopped garlic to taste....so easy!

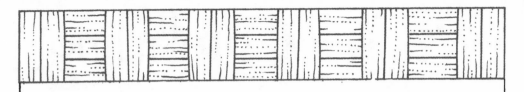

Easy Cornbread

Amy Robbins
Waupaca, WI

*Can also be baked the traditional way in
a well-seasoned cast iron skillet.*

1 c. all-purpose flour
1 c. cornmeal
3 T. sugar
1 T. baking powder

1/2 t. salt
2 eggs
1 c. milk
1/4 c. oil

Stir together flour, cornmeal, sugar, baking powder and salt in a
medium bowl; set aside. In another bowl, blend eggs, milk and oil.
Add flour mixture and stir until smooth; pour into a greased
9"x9" baking pan. Bake at 425 degrees for 20 to 25 minutes.
Serves 6 to 8.

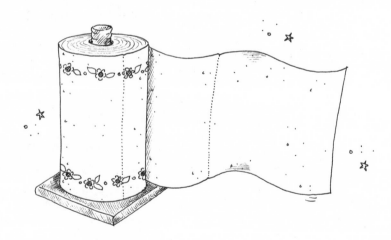

A wooden spindle makes a handy paper towel stand...simply
screw it onto a wooden base from the craft store.

4-Ingredient Biscuits

Debi DeVore
Dover, OH

Toss in some raisins, orange zest or even chocolate chips to make these biscuits extra-special.

8-oz. pkg. cream cheese, softened
2 c. all-purpose flour

1 T. baking powder
1/2 c. milk

Place cream cheese in a mixing bowl; set aside. Combine flour and baking powder in another bowl; cut into cream cheese until crumbly. Stir in milk to form a dough; pat onto a floured surface to 3/4-inch thick. Cut out 10 to 12 biscuits with a biscuit cutter or the top of a drinking glass. Arrange on a lightly greased baking sheet; bake at 425 degrees for 12 to 15 minutes, until golden. Makes one dozen.

It's easy to freshen up yesterday's crusty rolls or loaf of bread. Simply sprinkle with water and bake at 400 degrees for 6 to 8 minutes.

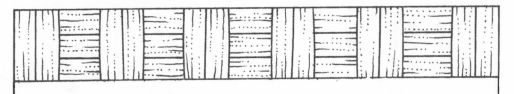

English Muffin Bread

Jane Silcox
West Salem, OH

*We love to toast this bread for breakfast...it's
delicious with butter and jam!*

2 envs. active dry yeast
6 c. all-purpose flour, divided
1 T. sugar
2 t. salt
1/4 t. baking soda
2 c. milk
1/2 c. water
2 to 3 T. cornmeal, divided

Combine yeast, 3 cups flour, sugar, salt and baking soda; set aside.
In a saucepan, heat milk and water until very warm but not boiling,
120 to 130 degrees on a cooking thermometer. Remove from heat
and add to dry mixture; mix well. Stir in remaining flour to make a
stiff batter. Sprinkle one to 2 tablespoons cornmeal into 2 greased
8"x4" loaf pans. Spoon batter into pans; sprinkle tops with remaining
cornmeal. Cover; let rise in a warm place for 45 minutes. Bake at
400 degrees for 25 minutes. Remove from pans immediately; let cool.
Slice and toast to serve; refrigerate any unused bread. Makes 2 loaves.

A crock of honey butter...so delicious on warm muffins. Simply
blend 1/2 cup each of honey and softened butter.

Warm & Comforting

Lavender Tea Bread

Leah Finks
Gooseberry Patch

A dainty bread that's perfect with a cup of tea.
Be sure to use lavender that's been processed as a
food product for use in cooking.

2 T. dried lavender
3/4 c. milk
2 c. all-purpose flour
1-1/2 t. baking powder

1/4 t. salt
1 c. sugar
6 T. butter, softened
2 eggs

Place lavender in a teaball or tie in a square of cheesecloth; place in a saucepan. Add milk and bring almost to a boil over medium heat. Remove pan from heat; let stand until cool, then discard lavender. Mix flour, baking powder and salt in a medium bowl. In another bowl, gradually add sugar to butter; add eggs one at a time, beating until light and fluffy. Add flour mixture alternately with lavender milk, in 3 parts. Mix until batter is just blended; do not overbeat. Pour into a greased 9"x5" loaf pan; bake at 325 degrees for 50 minutes, or until a toothpick comes out clean. Let cool in pan for 5 minutes; remove to a wire rack to finish cooling. Makes one loaf.

A small spice rack is just right for a
sweet collection of pie birds.

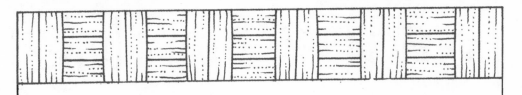

Dilly Beer Bread

Maria Kuhns
Crofton, MD

My family loves this bread, and it's oven-ready in 10 minutes!

3 c. self-rising flour
1-1/2 to 2-1/2 T. dill weed
3 T. sugar

12-oz. can beer
2 T. butter, melted

Mix flour, dill weed, sugar and beer; pour into a greased 9"x5" loaf pan. Drizzle with butter; bake at 350 degrees for one hour. Makes one loaf.

Create a children's reading corner. On a low table, next to a stack of cushy floor pillows, set out copies of the books you loved as a child, for a new generation to enjoy.

Come & Get It!

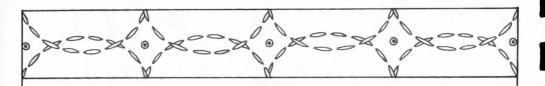

Chicken Dijon

Linda Patten
Lake Zurich, IL

This is my favorite way to serve chicken...I've been making it for over 20 years! Pounding the chicken flat makes it cook up fast.

4 boneless, skinless chicken
   breasts
2 T. all-purpose flour
1 T. butter
2 T. olive oil

2 T. lemon juice
2/3 c. chicken broth
1/2 c. white wine or
   chicken broth
1 T. Dijon mustard

Pound chicken breasts flat; sprinkle with flour and set aside. Melt butter and oil in a large skillet over medium-high heat. Add chicken; sauté until golden, about 3 to 4 minutes on each side. Reduce heat to low; sprinkle lemon juice over chicken. Cover and cook until chicken juices run clear, about 6 minutes. Place chicken on a serving dish; keep warm. Increase heat to high; add broth and wine or additional broth to skillet. Bring to a boil, stirring until liquid has been reduced by half. Reduce heat to low; stir in mustard and cook for one minute, until smooth. Pour sauce over chicken to serve. Makes 4 servings.

Stir some seasoned salt and coarse pepper into flour, then fill a
big shaker to keep by the side of the stove.
So handy to sprinkle on meat for pan-frying!

Come & Get It!

Mary's Swiss-Style Chicken

Mary Rita Schlagel
Warwick, NY

Add some steamed, buttered broccoli for a complete meal.

8 boneless, skinless chicken
   breasts
8 slices Swiss cheese
10-3/4 oz. can cream of
   chicken soup
1/2 c. dry white wine or
   chicken broth

1-1/2 c. chicken-flavored
   stuffing mix
1 apple, cored, peeled
   and chopped
1/4 c. butter, diced

Arrange chicken in a greased 13"x9" baking pan; top each with a slice of cheese. Set aside. Combine soup and wine or broth; pour over chicken. In another bowl, mix stuffing with apple; spoon over chicken. Dot with butter. Bake, covered, at 350 degrees for one hour. Serves 6 to 8.

Calendars are a wonderful source of pictures for framing. Choose a favorite page and pair with a mat of coordinated fabric, then pop into a frame. Quick, easy and so inexpensive that you can change pictures with each season!

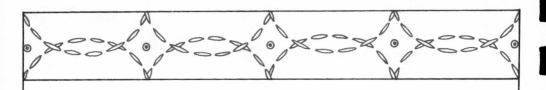

Southwest Slow-Cooker Chicken

Michelle Sheridan
Gooseberry Patch

This moist shredded chicken is great served over steamed rice or inside taco shells. Add hot salsa or jalapeños for extra kick!

15-oz. can corn, drained
16-oz. can black beans,
    drained and rinsed
16-oz. jar mild salsa
4 boneless, skinless chicken
    breasts

Garnish: shredded cheese,
    sour cream, sliced green
    onion, chopped red and
    yellow peppers

Layer three-quarters each of the corn and beans and half the salsa in a slow cooker. Arrange chicken over salsa; top with remaining corn, beans and salsa. Cover and cook on low setting for 8 hours. Remove chicken and shred; stir back into slow-cooker mixture. Add desired garnishes just before serving. Makes 4 to 6 servings.

Stack up several pieces of vintage luggage for a handy end table with hidden storage space. Use hand-me-down suitcases or tag sale finds...the more old travel stickers they have, the better!

Tomato & Green Chile Chicken

Denise Roberts
Crescent City, CA

The secret ingredient in this slow-cooker recipe is peanut butter!
It takes some of the heat out of the chiles.

4 to 6 boneless, skinless
   chicken breasts
3 14-1/2 oz. cans tomatoes
   with chiles

1/2 c. creamy peanut butter
prepared rice

Combine all ingredients except rice in a slow cooker. Cover and cook on low setting for 6 to 8 hours. Serve over rice. Makes 4 to 6 servings.

Create a cozy nook for yourself! A comfy chair and a table provide a quiet place for you to relax and read a book, write in a journal or just make a grocery list. Add a bowl of scented potpourri, if you like.

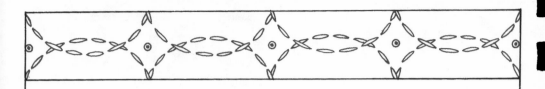

Slow-Cooker Turkey Breast

Linda Behling
Cecil, PA

This recipe makes the moistest turkey ever and your house will smell so delicious! I make it all year 'round...it's much too good to save for Thanksgiving only!

1/4 c. butter, melted
3/4 c. carrots, peeled and
   thickly sliced
1/2 c. celery, finely chopped
1/2 c. onion, finely chopped

2 T. fresh parsley, minced
3-1/2 to 4-lb. turkey breast
salt and pepper to taste
14-1/2 oz. can chicken broth

Combine butter, vegetables and parsley; spoon into center of slow cooker in a mound. Place turkey breast on top; sprinkle with salt and pepper to taste. Pour broth over all; cover and cook on low setting for 8 to 10 hours. Makes 6 to 8 servings.

Give your home a spicy holiday scent year 'round. Cover oranges with whole cloves, piercing the peel in circle and swirl designs or simply covering the fruit at random. Roll in cinnamon and ginger, then stack in a wooden bowl.

Come & Get It!

Creamed Chicken on Biscuits

Kathy Wyers
Cambridge, OH

A fast, tasty way to use up leftover chicken or turkey.

2 T. margarine
1/2 c. celery, chopped
1 T. green pepper, chopped
1-1/2 t. onion, chopped
1/4 c. all-purpose flour
1-1/2 c. chicken broth

1/2 c. milk
1-1/2 c. cooked chicken, diced
1/8 t. salt
8-oz. tube refrigerated biscuits,
   baked and split

Melt margarine in a large saucepan over medium heat; cook celery, pepper and onion until tender. Blend in flour; stir in broth and milk. Cook and stir over medium heat until smooth. Add chicken and salt; heat through. Spoon over biscuits to serve. Makes 8 servings.

A round, clear glass fish bowl makes a delightful centerpiece,
filled with colored sand and seashells or shiny ornament balls.

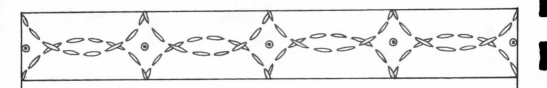

Italian Sweet Chicken

Michael Curry
Ardmore, OK

This scrumptious, quick recipe was handed down from my grandmother to my mother and then to me. My grandmother always used to make it with chicken wings.

1 lb. boneless, skinless chicken
   breasts, cut into strips
1 T. garlic salt
1 t. pepper

1/4 c. olive oil
24-oz. bottle catsup
3 c. water
1 c. brown sugar, packed

Sprinkle chicken with garlic salt and pepper; set aside. Heat oil in a large saucepan; add chicken. Cook over medium heat until golden, turning often. Empty catsup into a mixing bowl; pour water into catsup bottle, shake and pour into catsup. Add brown sugar; mix well. Pour mixture over chicken in pan. Stir well; lower heat, cover and simmer for at least one hour, until chicken is well-done and tender. Serves 4 to 6.

A simple lap quilt is a sweet way to preserve the memories in children's outgrown clothing. Cut large squares and stitch together, then layer with thin batting and a fabric backing.

Come & Get It!

Zippy Chicken Fingers

Marla Caldwell
Forest, IN

Mmm...great served with honey mustard or barbecue sauce for dipping!

4 boneless, skinless chicken
   breasts, cut into strips
juice of 1 lemon
poultry seasoning to taste

1-1/2 c. seasoned dry
   bread crumbs
1/4 c. oil

Place chicken strips in a bowl; sprinkle with lemon juice, then with poultry seasoning to taste. Spread bread crumbs in a shallow dish; coat each chicken strip with crumbs. Pour oil in a 13"x9" baking pan; arrange strips on top. Bake, uncovered, at 375 degrees for 20 minutes, turning once, until golden. Serves 4.

Turn old silver spoons and forks into tinkling windchimes. Use a craft drill to make a tiny hole in the end of each piece and hang with fishing line, or simply wind craft wire around the end. Decorate with glass beads if you wish, then hang around the edge of a tin pie plate or even an old pot lid.

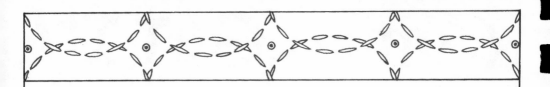

Herbed Chicken Casserole

Shirley Dine
Hilliard, OH

A main dish that's just right for carrying to new neighbors.

2-1/4 c. herbed stuffing
   mix, divided
1/2 c. butter, melted
1/2 c. chicken broth

2 c. cooked chicken, shredded
1 T. onion, grated
10-3/4 oz. can cream of
   celery soup

Toss together 1-3/4 cups stuffing and butter; add chicken broth, chicken and onion. Pour into a greased 13"x9" baking pan; spread soup over the top. Sprinkle with remaining stuffing; bake at 425 degrees for 15 minutes. Serves 4 to 6.

Set a narrow wooden flower box in a windowsill and plant a variety of flowering plants and herbs in it. Tuck a few whimsical pottery sit-abouts among the plants just for fun.

Easy Creamy Chicken Bake

Lisa Mand
Newburgh, IN

This is especially good served with brown rice.

4 boneless, skinless chicken
   breasts
salt and pepper to taste
10-3/4 oz. can cream of
   mushroom soup

1 pt. whipping cream
1/8 t. paprika
dried parsley to taste

Place chicken in a greased 13"x9" baking pan; sprinkle with salt and pepper. Set aside. Mix soup and cream together; pour over chicken. Sprinkle with paprika and parsley. Bake at 350 degrees for 1-1/4 hours. Serves 4.

Bright, colorful throw rugs or pillows are the quickest way to wake up a room!

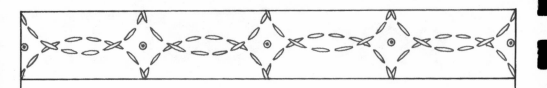

Chicken & Onions over Pasta

KimLisa Rizzo
Cedarhurst, NY

A flavorful recipe that's good enough for company.

2 T. oil
6 to 8 boneless, skinless
   chicken thighs
1 T. garlic powder
1 t. pepper
2 onions, sliced
3 to 4 c. water

6 cubes beef bouillon
1 t. dried oregano
8-oz. pkg. linguine pasta,
   cooked
Garnish: grated Parmesan
   cheese

Heat oil over medium heat in a large pot; add chicken and sauté until golden, about 15 to 20 minutes. Sprinkle chicken with garlic powder and pepper. Add onions to pot; sauté for 2 minutes. Add water to cover chicken; stir in bouillon cubes and oregano. Bring to a boil; lower heat, cover and simmer for 20 minutes. Uncover and simmer an additional 10 minutes. To serve, place cooked pasta in a deep serving bowl; pour chicken mixture over pasta. Let stand several minutes. Sprinkle with Parmesan cheese. Makes 6 to 8 servings.

Happy is...the family which can eat onions together.

-Charles Dudley Warner

Baked Italian Chicken

Fannie Troyer
Brinkhaven, OH

*This tasty recipe proves you can get dinner on the table
quickly without sacrificing flavor.*

1/2 c. grated Parmesan cheese
2 T. dried oregano
1 T. fresh parsley, minced
1/4 t. pepper
1/8 t. garlic powder

4 boneless, skinless chicken
   breasts
2 egg whites, beaten
1 T. margarine, melted

Combine Parmesan cheese and seasonings in a bowl; set aside.
Brush chicken with beaten egg whites; roll in Parmesan mixture.
Arrange in a 13"x9" baking pan sprayed with non-stick vegetable
spray. Drizzle with margarine. Bake, uncovered, at 425 degrees until
juices run clear, about 15 to 25 minutes. Makes 4 servings.

Make crystal sparkle...add a couple splashes of
vinegar to the wash water.

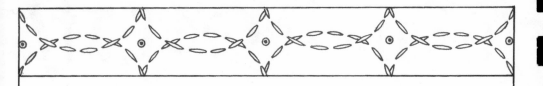

Oven-Fried Chicken

Jacque Moss
Grand Prairie, TX

Crisp golden chicken without the mess of stovetop frying.

1/4 c. butter
1/4 c. olive or peanut oil
1/2 c. all-purpose flour
1 t. salt

1 t. paprika
1/4 t. pepper
2-1/2 to 3 lbs. boneless,
     skinless chicken breasts

Melt butter and oil in a 13"x9" baking pan in a 425-degree oven;
set aside. Mix together flour, salt, paprika and pepper in a shallow
dish; dip chicken pieces into mixture. Arrange chicken in pan.
Lower oven to 325 degrees and bake for 60 minutes, turning once.
Serves 6 to 8.

Make a delicious honey-mustard dip for chicken nuggets with
2/3 cup honey and 1/3 cup mustard. Try different kinds of honey
and mustard to create flavor variations.

Come & Get It!

Lemon Pepper Chicken

Beverly Dowdell
Westerville, OH

This was my mother-in-law's recipe and one of my husband's favorites. I served this at a dinner party on a trip to Australia...now it's a big hit there too!

2 T. lemon pepper
1 T. seasoned salt
1-1/2 t. garlic salt
3 T. butter
1/4 c. olive oil

4 to 6 boneless, skinless
  chicken breasts
1 c. all-purpose flour
1/2 c. lemon juice
1/2 c. water

Mix together seasonings and set aside. Melt butter in a skillet over medium heat; add olive oil. Pat chicken dry; roll in flour. Add chicken to skillet and cook until golden on one side; sprinkle with half of seasoning mixture. Turn chicken; sprinkle on other side with remaining seasoning. Continue cooking until crusty and golden on both sides. Add lemon juice and water to skillet and simmer for 10 minutes. Arrange chicken in a lightly greased 13"x9" baking pan; spoon pan juices over top. Bake at 325 degrees for 45 minutes. Serves 4 to 6.

Add the final touch to a festive dinner table with small fruit for placecards. Letter a card with each guest's name and insert it in a slit in the top of the fruit. Shiny apples, yellow lemons or tiny pumpkins are all pleasing to the eye.

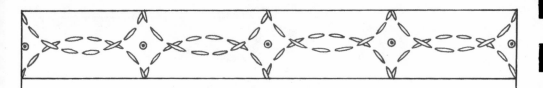

Bunny's Company Casserole

Brenda Derby
Northborough, MA

*This casserole can be layered, then refrigerated...bake it
a little longer until it's hot and bubbly.*

1 T. butter
1 lb. ground beef
2 8-oz. cans tomato sauce
1/8 t. sugar
8-oz. pkg. cream cheese,
   softened

8-oz. container cottage cheese
1/2 c. green onion, chopped
1 T. green pepper, minced
4 c. prepared elbow macaroni
Optional: 2 T. butter, melted

Melt butter in a skillet and sauté ground beef until browned; drain.
Add tomato sauce and sugar; remove from heat. Blend cheeses with
onion and green pepper; set aside. Spread half the macaroni in a
greased 2-quart casserole dish; cover with cheese mixture and mix
evenly. Add remaining macaroni; drizzle with melted butter, if desired,
and top with meat mixture. Bake, uncovered, for 30 to 45 minutes at
375 degrees. Serves 4 to 6.

Change the mood of your table setting with a runner! Look for
fun prints at the fabric store...it only takes one or 2 yards,
simply hemmed or pinked. Or use unexpected fabrics like a long
plaid winter scarf or a summery beach towel.

Come & Get It!

Hamburger Heaven

Karen Brandenburg
Springfield, MO

A hearty meal in one skillet.

1 lb. ground beef
8-oz. pkg. American cheese
   slices
1 c. celery, chopped
2-1/4 oz. can sliced black
   olives, drained

2 c. fine egg noodles, uncooked
14-1/2 oz. can stewed tomatoes
1/2 c. water

Brown beef in a large skillet; drain and return to skillet. Layer remaining ingredients except water over beef in order given. Pour water over all. Cover; simmer for 30 minutes, or until noodles are tender. Serves 4.

A vintage wooden soda crate makes a clever shadow box for an assortment of small treasures. Freshen it up with paint or leave it as is for rustic charm.

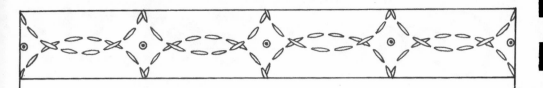

Family's Favorite Lasagna

JoAnne Hayon
Sheboygan, WI

My husband says this lasagna is the best!
I've been making it since we were married in 1977.

1 lb. ground beef
1/2 c. onion, chopped
6-oz. can tomato paste
20-oz. can diced tomatoes
1-1/2 t. dried oregano
1-1/4 t. garlic powder
1 t. salt

3/4 t. pepper
8-oz. pkg. lasagna, cooked
8-oz. pkg. shredded mozzarella
  cheese
12-oz. container cottage cheese
Garnish: grated Parmesan
  cheese

Combine ground beef and onion in a large skillet over medium heat; brown and drain. Add tomato paste, tomatoes and seasonings; reduce heat and simmer for 20 minutes. In a greased 11"x7" baking pan, layer lasagna, cheeses and meat sauce. Repeat layers, ending with sauce; sprinkle with Parmesan cheese. Bake at 350 degrees for 30 minutes. Let stand several minutes; cut into squares to serve. Makes 6 to 8 servings.

Add a ribbon hanger to framed pictures for a finishing touch.

Come & Get It!

String Pie

Tammy McCartney
Oxford, OH

*This recipe is always popular at potlucks. It's also a good
main dish to deliver to a family with a new baby...tuck in
a loaf of garlic bread and a bag of salad greens.*

1 lb. ground beef
1/2 c. onion, chopped
1/2 c. green pepper, chopped
15-1/2 oz. jar spaghetti sauce
8-oz. pkg. spaghetti, cooked
1/3 c. grated Parmesan cheese

2 eggs, beaten
2 T. butter, melted
8-oz. container cottage cheese
1/2 c. shredded mozzarella
 cheese

Cook beef, onion and green pepper in large skillet until browned.
Drain; stir in sauce and set aside. In a large bowl, mix spaghetti,
Parmesan cheese, eggs and butter. Spread in a greased 13"x9" baking
pan; spread cottage cheese over the top. Pour sauce mixture over
cottage cheese; sprinkle with mozzarella cheese. Bake at 350 degrees
for about 20 minutes. Serves 6 to 8.

A fabric-skirted round table fits easily in an odd corner...simply
top it with a big circle of fabric. Underneath, lots of storage
space is hidden away.

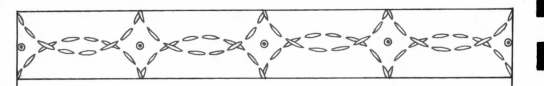

Skillet Goulash

Kari Hodges
Jacksonville, TX

I like to serve cornbread with this old family favorite.

2 lbs. ground beef
6 potatoes, peeled and diced
14-1/2 oz. can ranch-style
   beans
15-1/4 oz. can corn, drained

14-1/2 oz. can tomatoes
   with chiles
15-oz. can tomato sauce
salt and pepper to taste

Brown ground beef over medium heat in a large Dutch oven; drain. Add remaining ingredients; reduce heat. Simmer until potatoes are tender and mixture is thick, about 45 minutes. Makes 8 to 10 servings.

The base of a tall butter churn makes a clever umbrella stand.

Come & Get It!

Slow-Cooker Smothered Steak

Zoe Groff
Lebanon, TN

This hearty dish is sure to be a hit at any dinner party...and they'll never know it only took you 10 minutes to put it together!

1 to 1-1/2 lbs. beef chuck or
    round steak, cut into
    bite-size pieces
1/3 c. all-purpose flour
1/4 t. pepper
1 onion, sliced

1 green pepper, sliced
14-1/2 oz. can diced tomatoes
4-oz. can sliced mushrooms,
    drained
3 T. soy sauce
prepared rice

Place meat in slow cooker. Sprinkle with flour and pepper; stir well to coat meat. Add remaining ingredients except rice. Cover and cook on high setting for one hour; reduce to low setting and cook for 8 hours. Serve over cooked rice. Makes 4 to 6 servings.

Look for postcard reproductions of favorite paintings and place in small frames for a display to enliven a corner. Scatter tiny mirrors around the grouping to catch the light.

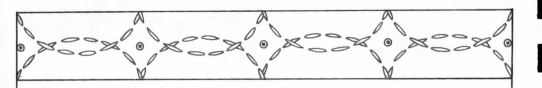

Easy Cabbage Casserole

Gayle Daniel
Danville, VA

Great comfort food on a cold night!

1 onion, sliced
1 T. oil
2 lbs. ground beef

1 head cabbage, shredded
2 10-3/4 oz. cans tomato soup
salt and cayenne pepper to taste

In a skillet over medium heat, sauté onion in oil. Add ground beef and cook until browned; drain. Layer beef mixture with cabbage in a lightly greased 13"x9" baking pan. Top with soup; sprinkle to taste with salt and cayenne pepper. Cover tightly with aluminum foil. Bake at 350 degrees for one hour and 15 minutes, until cabbage is fork-tender. Serves 6 to 8.

Make your own potpourri...preserve the sweet scent of bouquets you've received. Scatter petals on paper towels and let dry for several days until paper-crisp. Mix in some whole cinnamon or cloves and a few drops of scented oil, then place in a pretty dish or lidded jar.

German Skillet

Ruth Fangman
Louisville, KY

A nice fix & forget recipe for company.

1 lb. ground beef	1 onion, sliced
1 T. butter	1-1/4 t. salt
14-oz. can sauerkraut	1/4 t. pepper
2/3 c. instant rice, uncooked	8-oz. can tomato sauce

Brown ground beef in a skillet over medium heat; drain and set aside.
Melt butter in skillet over low heat; add sauerkraut. Sprinkle rice over
sauerkraut; top with onion and beef. Sprinkle with salt and pepper;
top with tomato sauce. Cover and simmer over low heat for 25 to
30 minutes. Serves 4 to 6.

March a collection of herb plants in tiny pots across the kitchen
windowsill...oh-so sweet and handy for last-minute seasoning.

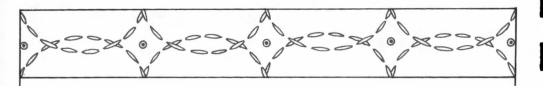

Zucchini Casserole

Janice Hunn
Lynwood, IL

Whenever I make this, it reminds me of our family reunions. Every year, Aunt Camila made this with fresh vegetables from her garden. It was always the first buffet dish to be emptied.

1 lb. ground beef
1/2 c. onion, chopped
1/2 c. celery, chopped
1/2 c. green pepper, chopped
3 T. oil
3 c. zucchini, sliced 1/8-inch
   thick
1/2 t. garlic salt

1/2 t. dried oregano
1/2 t. dried basil
1/4 t. Italian seasoning
1/4 t. pepper
28-oz. can stewed tomatoes,
   chopped
1-1/2 c. shredded Cheddar
   cheese

Brown ground beef in a large skillet; drain and remove from skillet. Sauté onion, celery and green pepper in oil in skillet until tender. Layer zucchini and ground beef in skillet over vegetable mixture; do not stir. Blend seasonings and sprinkle over top, followed by tomatoes; do not stir. Simmer, uncovered, over low heat until all liquid has evaporated, about 30 to 45 minutes. Remove from heat; sprinkle cheese on top. Cover and let stand until cheese melts. Serves 4 to 6.

Arrange several small potted herbs on a tray for a centerpiece with a fresh look and fragrance.

Pepper Steak

Amy Allen
Anderson, IN

A favorite recipe from my husband's mom.

2 T. cornstarch	1 lb. beef round steak or sirloin,
1-1/2 c. plus 2 T. water, divided	cut into strips
3 T. oil, divided	2 green peppers, cut into strips
1 T. soy sauce	2 T. garlic, pressed
1/8 t. pepper	1-1/2 c. prepared rice

Combine cornstarch, 2 tablespoons water, one tablespoon oil,
soy sauce and pepper in a bowl; stir in beef strips and set aside.
Heat one tablespoon oil in a wok or large skillet; sauté green peppers
over medium heat until tender-crisp. Remove peppers from skillet;
set aside. Add remaining oil to skillet; add garlic and sauté until
golden. Add beef mixture to skillet; cook for one minute without
stirring. Cook and stir until meat is cooked medium-rare; remove from
skillet. Add remaining water; bring to a boil. Remove from heat and
stir in cooked rice. Top with beef and peppers; cover and let stand for
at least 5 minutes before serving. Serves 4 to 6.

A big shaker of seasoning salt is a must-have for tasty grilling.
Mix up your very own blend! A good basic mixture is a teaspoon
each of salt, pepper, garlic powder and oregano or rosemary.
Like it spicy? Add some cayenne pepper or dry mustard.

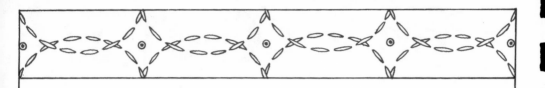

Barbecued Steak

Sharon Crider
Lebanon, MO

Steak is so luscious and tender when prepared this way.

1 c. catsup
1/2 c. water
1/4 c. vinegar
1/2 c. onion, chopped
1-1/2 T. Worcestershire sauce
1 T. mustard

2 T. brown sugar, packed
1/2 t. salt
1/8 t. pepper
4 lbs. beef round steak, cut into
   serving-size portions

Combine all ingredients except meat in a saucepan. Bring to a boil; lower heat and simmer gently for about 5 minutes. Keep warm. Pound meat to tenderize; arrange in a lightly greased large roasting pan. Pour sauce over meat. Cover tightly; bake at 325 degrees for 1-1/2 to 2 hours, or until meat is fork-tender. Makes 8 to 10 servings.

A quick & easy side dish...quarter new potatoes and toss with a little olive oil, salt and pepper. Spread on a baking sheet and bake at 400 degrees until crisp and golden, 35 to 40 minutes.

Come & Get It!

Beef Porcupine Meatballs

Terri Lock
Waverly, MO

As a teacher, I need fast home-style meals to serve to my family of 5 before I leave for evening school events. They love these meatballs!

8-oz. pkg. beef-flavored rice
   vermicelli mix, divided
1 lb. ground beef

1 egg, beaten
2-1/2 c. water
prepared egg noodles

Combine rice vermicelli mix with ground beef and egg, setting aside seasoning packet from mix. Shape into small meatballs; brown on all sides in a skillet. Drain. Combine contents of seasoning packet with water; pour over meatballs. Cover and simmer over low heat for 30 minutes. Serve meatballs and sauce over cooked egg noodles. Makes 4 to 6 servings.

Re-cover the dining room chair seats...it's a snap! Simply remove seats with a screwdriver, wrap with fabric and use a stapler to tack down folded-under edges. Set in place and reinsert screws.

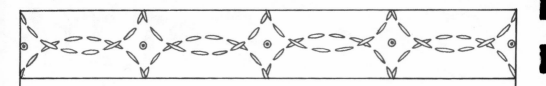

3-Cheese Baked Penne

Vickie

It's fun to make this hearty casserole with a mix of pastas like ziti, rotini and shells.

1 lb. ground beef
1 lb. ground sweet Italian
   sausage
1 onion, chopped
2 26-oz. jars spaghetti sauce
16-oz. pkg. penne pasta, cooked
   and divided

8-oz. pkg. sliced provolone
   cheese
1 c. sour cream
8-oz. pkg. shredded mozzarella
   cheese
Garnish: grated Parmesan
   cheese

Brown beef, sausage and onion together in a large skillet over medium heat; drain. Add spaghetti sauce to skillet and simmer over low heat for 15 minutes. Layer as follows in a greased 13"x9" baking pan; half of pasta, provolone cheese, sour cream, half of sauce mixture, remaining pasta, mozzarella cheese and remaining sauce. Top with grated Parmesan cheese. Bake at 350 degrees for 30 minutes, or until hot and bubbly. Serves 6 to 8.

Set a leaf placecard at each dinner guest's place. Write each name on a leaf using a gold or silver pen...try bright green leaves in summer, beautiful red or orange fallen leaves in autumn.

Come & Get It!

Chili-Cheese Dog Casserole

Lesli Saacks-Holyfield
Virginia Beach, VA

The kids can't get enough of this!

8-oz. tube refrigerated
   buttermilk biscuits
1/2 c. shredded Cheddar cheese

8 hot dogs
15-oz. can chili with beans

Flatten each biscuit into a 6-inch round; sprinkle with cheese.
Place a hot dog near the edge of each round; roll up. Place seam-side
down in a greased 13"x9" baking pan; bake at 375 degrees for
18 to 20 minutes. Top with chili; bake for an additional 5 minutes,
until heated through. Serves 8.

Tabletop topiaries are easy to make. Push a foam ball onto one
end of a dowel, then push the other end into a foam-filled pot.
Cover the ball with craft glue and roll it in sphagnum moss or
even dried herbs. Decorate as you like with silk flowers, ribbons
or strings of beads.

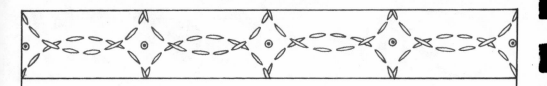

Sunday Pork Roast

Teri Eklund
Olympia, WA

Toss some new potatoes with olive oil and bake in a separate pan alongside the roast.

1-1/2 to 2-lb. pork loin roast
1 sweet onion, thinly sliced
1/4 t. dried sage
1/4 t. pepper
3/4 c. apple juice

3 T. soy sauce
1/4 c. water
1/4 c. brown sugar, packed
2 cloves garlic, minced

Place roast in a lightly greased roasting pan. Arrange onion slices over roast; sprinkle with sage and pepper. Combine remaining ingredients in a small bowl; pour into roasting pan. Cover pan with aluminum foil and bake for one hour at 350 degrees; uncover and bake for an additional 15 minutes. Serve roast sliced, topped with onions and some of the pan juices. Makes 6 to 8 servings.

Melted wax pops right out of candleholders when they're placed in the freezer for a couple of hours.

Come & Get It!

Barbecued Pork Chops

Shirley Flanagan
Wooster, OH

My mom gave me this easy, tasty recipe.

6 pork chops
3/4 c. catsup
1 t. celery seed

1/2 t. dry mustard
1/2 t. ground cloves

Arrange pork chops in a large skillet; add water to cover bottom of skillet. Over medium heat, brown chops on both sides. Combine remaining ingredients and spread over both sides of chops. Cover and cook over low heat for 20 minutes, until tender. Serves 6.

Show off prized cookie cutters....store them
in a big glass canister.

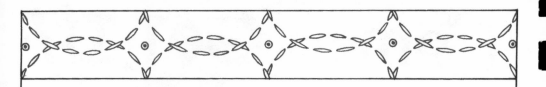

Stuffed Spaghetti Pie

Kathy Carroll
Imperial, MO

Add a big tossed salad and a basket of garlic bread...presto,
a delicious, easy-to-serve dinner for guests.

1 c. cottage cheese
3/4 c. grated Parmesan cheese
2 eggs, beaten
1 clove garlic, minced
1/2 t. dried basil
1/2 t. dried oregano

16-oz. pkg. spaghetti, cooked
1 lb. ground sausage
1 c. onion, chopped
8-oz. pkg. shredded mozzarella
 cheese, divided
26-oz. jar spaghetti sauce

In a large bowl, combine cottage cheese, Parmesan cheese, eggs, garlic, herbs and spaghetti; toss to coat spaghetti. Set aside. In a skillet, cook sausage and onion until browned; drain. Press half of spaghetti mixture into a greased 9" round springform pan. Sprinkle with 1/2 cup mozzarella cheese; top with sausage mixture. Press remaining spaghetti mixture on top; top with remaining mozzarella cheese. Bake at 350 degrees for 30 to 35 minutes. Remove from oven; warm sauce and spread over top. Let stand 10 to 15 minutes; remove sides of springform pan and cut into wedges. Serves 8.

Turn plain fingertip towels into something special...simply stitch on embroidered trim.

Come & Get It!

Mike's Slow-Cooker Italian Chops

Leslie McKinley
Macomb, MO

My dad is a master at cooking meats! We enjoy these chops with buttered noodles, rice or couscous.

5 pork chops
1-1/2 onions, coarsely chopped
15-oz. can stewed tomatoes
1/3 c. oil
1-1/2 t. Italian seasoning

1-1/2 t. garlic powder
2 t. smoke-flavored cooking
   sauce
1/4 c. water

Layer chops and onions in a slow cooker; pour remaining ingredients on top. Cover and cook on low setting for 3 to 4 hours, until tender. Makes 5 servings.

The simplest table decorations are often the prettiest! Try filling a primitive wooden bowl with shiny red apples or fragrant yellow lemons for the kitchen table, or pile the bowl with bright-colored balls of yarn for a crafting corner.

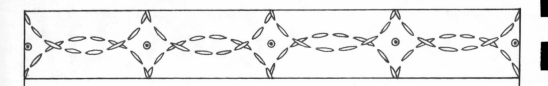

Slow-Cooker Hawaiian Ham

*Satoko Harjo
Edmonds, WA*

*My friends and I get together every 6 to 8 weeks and exchange
frozen dinners. Hawaiian Ham is the most-requested main dish!*

2 lbs. cooked ham, thinly sliced
1/4 c. onion, chopped
1 c. catsup
1/2 c. water
1/2 c. vinegar
1/4 c. mustard

1/4 c. plus 2 T. brown sugar,
   packed
2 T. Worcestershire sauce
8 Kaiser rolls, split
15-1/4 oz. can pineapple
   slices, drained

Combine all ingredients except rolls and pineapple in a slow cooker.
Cover and cook on low setting for 6 to 8 hours. Serve ham on split
rolls, topped with pineapple slices. Serves 8.

Place favorite collectibles or whimsical objects around a room in
groups of 3 to 5 for the most eye-catching arrangement.

Come & Get It!

Peach-Glazed Pork Chops

Cathey Farmer
Lake George, CO

Another mouthwatering slow-cooker main dish...it doesn't get easier or tastier than this!

6 boneless pork chops
8-1/2 oz. can sliced peaches,
   drained and juice reserved
1/4 c. butter, softened

6-oz. pkg. herb-flavored
   stuffing mix
1/3 c. peach preserves
1 T. Dijon mustard

Lightly brown pork chops in a skillet sprayed with non-stick vegetable spray; do not overcook. Set aside. Combine reserved peach juice with enough hot water to measure 1-1/2 cups; pour into a large bowl. Add butter; heat in the microwave, stirring occasionally, until butter is melted. Stir in stuffing mix and peaches; spoon half the stuffing mixture into a slow cooker. Arrange chops over top. Combine preserves and mustard; spread over chops. Top with remaining stuffing mixture. Cover and cook on high setting for 40 minutes, or until chops are no longer pink. Serves 6.

A comfortable house is a great source of happiness.
It ranks immediately after health and a good conscience.

–Sydney Smith

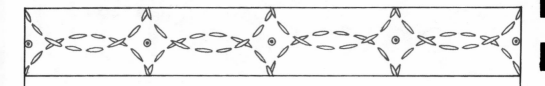

Aunt Velma's Hamloaf

Kimberly Bernat
Miramar, FL

*Ask your butcher to grind the smoked ham for you...if this
isn't possible, a food processor works equally well.*

2/3 to 1 c. brown sugar, packed
1/4 to 1/3 c. vinegar
1 to 1-1/2 T. dry mustard
1-1/2 lbs. smoked ham, ground
1 lb. ground pork

2 eggs, beaten
1 sleeve saltine crackers,
   crushed
1/2 c. water

Whisk together brown sugar, vinegar, and mustard in a small bowl;
set aside. In a large bowl, mix together meats, eggs and cracker
crumbs. Form into a loaf shape; place on a rack in a lightly greased
roasting pan. Pour water into bottom of pan; baste with half of brown
sugar mixture. Bake at 350 degrees for one hour; turn loaf over and
baste with remaining brown sugar mixture. Bake for an additional
hour at 350 degrees. Serves 6 to 8.

A weathered ladder
makes a useful and
unexpected display. Hang
folded quilts over the rungs
in the living room or use as a
holder for big fluffy towels
in the bath.

Come & Get It!

Sweet & Hot Peppered Pork on Rice

Debbie Byrne
Clinton, CT

We love this recipe...it's a little sweet, a little spicy.
Dinner is on the table in 20 minutes!

1/4 c. brown sugar, packed	1/4 t. salt
1/2 t. red pepper flakes	1/8 t. pepper
2 T. soy sauce	1 red onion, sliced
1 lb. pork tenderloin, cut into strips	prepared rice

Mix together brown sugar, pepper flakes and soy sauce in a small bowl; set aside. Spray a large skillet with non-stick vegetable spray; heat over medium-high heat. Add pork; sprinkle with salt and pepper. Cook and stir until pork is nearly done; add onion and cook an additional 3 minutes. Pour brown sugar mixture into skillet; heat through. Serve over cooked rice. Makes 3 to 4 servings.

Trim a grapevine wreath for a welcoming gift! For the new neighbors, tie on coupons and cards from area businesses. For new parents, attach rattles, tiny baby toiletries and a baby spoon. Or welcome a new kitten...wind bright-colored yarn around the wreath and tie on catnip mice.

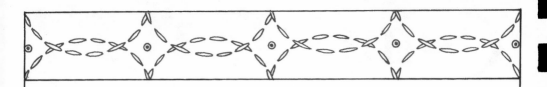

BBQ Pork Sandwiches

Cyndi Jones
Albany, OH

*Perfect for a summer get-together...the slow cooker does
the work and the kitchen stays cool!*

2 yellow onions, sliced and
    separated into rings
4-lb. boneless pork roast,
    trimmed and halved
garlic powder, pepper and
    seasoning salt to taste

1 c. cola
22-oz. bottle barbecue sauce
6 hamburger buns or Kaiser
    rolls, split and toasted

The day before serving, place half the onion rings in a slow cooker;
set aside. Sprinkle roast halves with seasonings; arrange over onion
rings and top with remaining onions. Pour cola over roast. Cover and
cook on low setting for 8 to 10 hours or overnight, until pork is very
tender. Remove pork from slow cooker and shred, using 2 forks.
Drain drippings from onion rings in slow cooker; return pork to cooker
and add sauce. Mix well; cover and cook an additional 2 hours on low
setting. Serve on buns or rolls. Makes 6 servings.

Every country home needs a
rocking chair for cuddling with
a child or whiling away an
afternoon. Turn an ordinary
rocker into an instant heirloom
with a coat of soft country blue
or autumn gold paint. Add a
plump pillow for comfort.

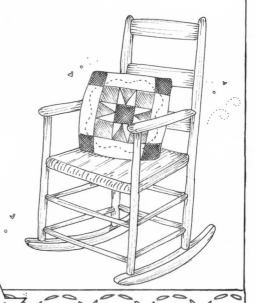

Ham & Cheddar Bake Supreme

Jo Ann

We enjoy this satisfying one-pan meal for brunch or dinner.

6 slices bread, divided
2.8-oz. can French fried
    onions, divided
8-oz. pkg. shredded Cheddar
    cheese
1/2 lb. cooked ham, chopped

10-oz. pkg. frozen chopped
    broccoli, thawed
5 eggs
2 c. milk
1/2 t. dry mustard
1/4 t. pepper

Cube 3 slices bread; arrange in a greased 12"x8" baking pan. Top with
half the onions and all the cheese, ham and broccoli. Slice remaining
bread in half diagonally. Arrange bread down center of casserole,
overlapping slightly, with crusted points all in one direction. Set aside.
Beat together eggs, milk and seasonings; pour over top. Bake,
uncovered, at 325 degrees for one hour and 10 minutes until center
is firm. Top with remaining onions; bake an additional 5 minutes.
Let stand 10 minutes before serving. Serves 6 to 8.

Plant herb seedlings in the pockets of a big terra cotta
strawberry jar. Set it outside the kitchen door for a pinch of
fresh herbs anytime!

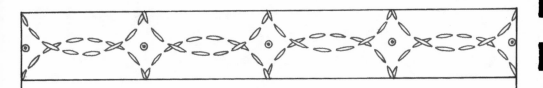

Sweet & Spicy Pork Chops

Pam Fowler
Newnan, GA

*These chops are so delectable, you just
might want to double the recipe!*

5 T. oil, divided
4 boneless pork chops
2 cloves garlic, minced
1/2 c. red wine or beef broth
1/2 c. soy sauce

1/4 c. brown sugar, packed
1/2 t. red pepper flakes
4 t. cornstarch
1/4 c. water
prepared linguine pasta

Heat one tablespoon oil over medium heat in a skillet; add pork chops.
Cook until browned; remove from skillet. Stir garlic into pan drippings;
heat until golden. Return pork chops to pan; lower heat. In a bowl,
combine wine or broth, soy sauce, brown sugar, pepper flakes and
remaining oil; pour over chops. Cover and simmer for 40 minutes,
turning once. Remove chops from skillet; set aside. Mix cornstarch
and water; add to sauce in skillet. Heat and stir until thickened.
Serve chops and sauce over linguine. Serves 4.

Kids will be happy
to hang up coats and
backpacks on their own
special peg! Mount a row
of wooden pegs on the
wall, low enough for
children to reach. Label
each with a child's
name...no more fuss
when getting ready to
leave for school!

Susie | Mary Jo | Patti

Come & Get It!

BBQ Pork Ribs

Diane Gregori
Riverside, CA

*A big platter of corn on the cob is the perfect partner
for these juicy ribs.*

3 qts. water
4 lbs. pork ribs, cut into
    serving portions

1 onion, quartered
2 t. salt
1/4 t. pepper

Bring water to a boil in a large pot; place ribs, onion, salt and pepper in water. Reduce heat, cover and simmer for 1-1/2 hours. Remove ribs from pot; drain. Grill ribs for 10 minutes on each side, brushing frequently with BBQ Sauce, until tender. Serves 4 to 6.

BBQ Sauce:

1/2 c. vinegar
1/2 c. brown sugar, packed
1/2 c. chili sauce
1/4 c. Worcestershire sauce
2 T. onion, chopped

1 T. lemon juice
1/2 t. dry mustard
1/8 t. garlic powder
1/8 t. cayenne pepper

Combine all ingredients in a small saucepan. Simmer over low heat, uncovered, for one hour.

Having a picnic on a breezy day? Cast-off clip earrings make sparkly tablecloth weights...simply clip 'em to the 4 corners of the cloth.

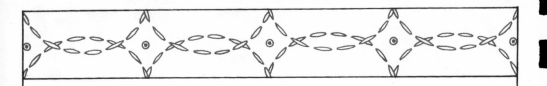

Spinach-Stuffed Shells

Penny McShane
Lombard, IL

Top the shells with your family's choice of pasta sauce.

15-oz. container ricotta cheese
8-oz. pkg. shredded mozzarella
   cheese
10-oz. pkg. frozen chopped
   spinach, thawed and
   drained

1 egg, beaten
1/2 t. onion powder
1/4 t. nutmeg
12-oz. pkg. jumbo pasta
   shells, cooked
28-oz. jar spaghetti sauce

Stir together cheeses, spinach, egg and seasonings in a large bowl.
Spoon mixture into cooked shells; arrange in a greased 13"x9" baking
pan. Pour sauce over top; cover and bake for 45 minutes at
350 degrees. Serves 6.

Plant a butterfly garden in a sunny corner of the yard! Milkweed,
bee balm and shasta daisies are some good flower choices...add
a shallow pan of water for butterflies to drink from.

Come & Get It!

Baked Ziti with Spinach & Cheese

Karen Pilcher
Burleson, TX

Penne and mostaccioli pasta work well in this recipe too.

2 10-oz. pkgs. frozen chopped
   spinach
3 eggs, beaten
15-oz. container ricotta cheese
2/3 c. grated Parmesan cheese
1/4 t. pepper

16-oz. pkg. ziti pasta, cooked
27-1/2 oz. jar spaghetti sauce
2 t. dried oregano
12-oz. pkg. shredded mozzarella
   cheese

Cook spinach as package directs; drain, cool and squeeze out well.
Add eggs, ricotta cheese, Parmesan cheese and pepper; mix well
and set aside. Combine cooked ziti with sauce and oregano. Place
half the ziti mixture in a lightly greased 13"x9" baking pan; layer
with mozzarella and spinach mixture. Add remaining ziti mixture;
cover with aluminum foil. Bake at 375 degrees for 25 minutes, or until
bubbly. Let stand about 10 minutes before serving. Makes 8 servings.

Drape a charm bracelet
around a crystal candle
holder...the charms will
sparkle with candlelight.

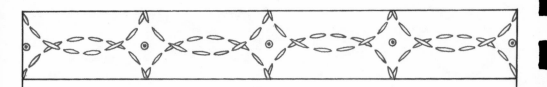

Summer Linguine

Lisa Sharman
Valencia, CA

A fresh, simple pasta dish...my teenage daughter loves it.

2 14-1/2 oz. cans diced
   tomatoes, drained
1 bunch green onions, chopped
2 cloves garlic, pressed
1 bunch fresh basil, chopped
salt and pepper to taste

8-oz. pkg. mozzarella cheese,
   cubed
16-oz. pkg. linguine pasta,
   uncooked
3 to 4 T. olive oil

Combine tomatoes, onions, garlic, seasonings and mozzarella in a
large serving bowl; mix well and set aside. Cook pasta according to
package directions; drain and return to pan. Stir oil into pasta; add
pasta to mixture in bowl and toss to mix. Serves 6 to 8.

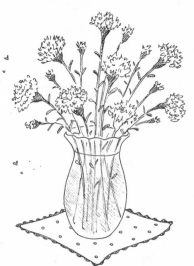

Make white flowers magically turn red, yellow
or blue! Drop a little food coloring into the water and plain white
carnations or Queen Anne's lace will gradually absorb the color.
Fun for kids to watch!

Vegetable Lo Mein à la Rob

*Robbin Chamberlain
Worthington, OH*

A savory main dish that's much easier than it looks...chop the veggies, stir up the sauce, and it goes together very quickly.

2 8-oz. pkgs. rice noodles, cooked
2 T. plus 1 t. sesame oil, divided
1/2 t. salt
1 onion, halved and sliced into crescents
2 stalks celery, thinly sliced
2 cloves garlic, pressed

1-1/2 t. fresh ginger, peeled and shredded
1 carrot, peeled and shredded
1 c. sliced mushrooms
1/4 lb. snow peas
1 c. corn
Optional: dry white wine or vegetable broth

Toss noodles in a bowl with one teaspoon sesame oil and salt; set aside. Heat remaining oil in a skillet over high heat. Add vegetables one at a time in order given; stir-fry each for 2 to 4 minutes until crisp-tender. Add a little white wine or vegetable broth to skillet if skillet gets too dry. Pour noodles on top and reduce heat to low. Drizzle sauce over noodles and toss all together. Serves 10 to 12.

Sauce:

1-1/2 T. cornstarch
4 T. sugar
6 T. soy sauce
1/2 c. dry white wine or vegetable broth

4 t. hoisin sauce
2 t. sesame oil
1 t. rice wine vinegar or white vinegar

Combine all ingredients in a small saucepan. Cook over low heat for 5 minutes, until thickened. Keep warm.

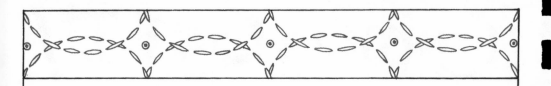

Maryland Crab Cakes

Karen Thomas
Princess Anne, MD

A true Maryland summer treat...top with a dollop of mayonnaise if you like. Crab cakes make scrumptious sandwiches too.

1 lb. crabmeat, flaked
3 T. mayonnaise
1 c. saltine cracker crumbs
1 t. seafood seasoning or pepper

1 t. mustard
2 t. Worcestershire sauce
1 egg, beaten
oil for frying

Mix all ingredients together except oil; form into 8 patties. Heat a small amount of oil in a skillet over medium heat; fry until golden on both sides. Drain on paper towels. Serves 8.

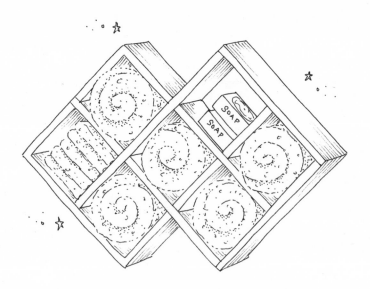

A folding wine rack is handy for holding fluffy towels in the bath...roll them up and place one in each opening.

Come & Get It!

Cheesy Tuna Tempter

Charity Meyer
Lewisberry, PA

*I took plain old tuna casserole and punched it up with
lots of cheese...now my daughter loves it!*

1/2 c. celery, chopped
1/4 c. onion, chopped
5 T. butter, divided
10-3/4 oz. can cream of
   mushroom soup
1-1/2 c. milk, divided
6-oz. can tuna, drained
1 c. finely shredded sharp
   Cheddar cheese

1/2 c. grated Parmesan cheese
1/4 t. salt
1/4 t. pepper
8-oz. pkg. medium egg noodles,
   cooked
1/2 c. round buttery crackers,
   crushed

In a large skillet over medium heat, sauté celery and onion in
2 tablespoons butter until tender. Add soup, milk, tuna, cheeses,
salt and pepper; mix well. Place noodles in a 2-quart casserole dish.
Pour mixture over top; toss to coat noodles. Sprinkle crumbs on top
and dot with remaining butter, cubed. Bake at 350 degrees for
25 minutes, or until hot and bubbly. Serves 4 to 6.

Put cut-glass coasters to new use as holders for
fat pillar candles...group several together for a glowing
centerpiece in an instant.

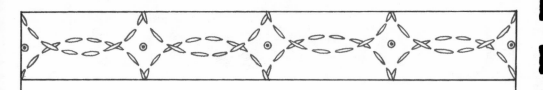

Seaside Linguine

Cathy Hillier
Gulf Breeze, FL

A luscious dish for seafood lovers.

1 clove garlic, chopped
1/4 c. butter
1 c. whipping cream
1/2 lb. crabmeat
1/2 lb. cooked tiny shrimp

1 c. grated Parmesan cheese
salt and pepper to taste
2 9-oz. pkgs. refrigerated
  linguine, cooked
Garnish: fresh parsley, chopped

Sauté garlic in butter in a large skillet over medium heat until tender. Stir in cream; cook until thickened, about 5 minutes. Add crabmeat, shrimp, cheese, salt and pepper. Reduce heat to low; cook for 2 to 3 minutes, until heated through. Transfer cooked linguine to a serving platter, top with seafood sauce and garnish with parsley. Serves 6.

Baskets are indispensible for storing toiletries and fresh towels in the bath. Decorate them creatively by hot gluing on buttons, seashells, wooden cut-outs or tiny trinkets around the top.

Linguine & Clams

Eleanor Moore
Newtown Square, PA

A delicious restaurant favorite...sprinkle with grated Parmesan for even more flavor.

2 T. olive oil
2 T. butter
3 cloves garlic, minced
2 10-oz. cans minced clams
1 t. dried oregano

1/3 c. white wine or chicken broth
2 T. fresh parsley, chopped
16-oz. pkg. linguine pasta, cooked

Heat oil and butter over medium heat in a skillet. Add garlic and cook until softened. Add clams with juice, oregano and wine or broth; heat for 5 minutes. Stir in parsley; serve over cooked linguine. Serves 6 to 8.

Fill glass snifters with jelly beans, candy corn, glass marbles or beach pebbles and insert a tea light in the center for a pretty seasonal setting.

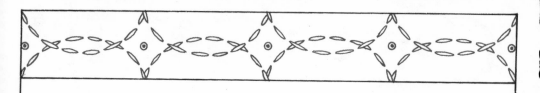

Baked Salmon Patties

Lisa Bownas
Gooseberry Patch

An old-fashioned quick & easy dinner that's still tasty.

14-3/4 oz. can salmon,
    drained and flaked
1 c. soft bread crumbs
1/2 c. green onion, diced

1 egg, beaten
2 T. lemon juice
1 t. Worcestershire sauce

Mix all ingredients together; shape into 4 patties. Place on a greased baking sheet; bake at 400 degrees for 5 to 6 minutes. Turn; bake an additional 5 to 6 minutes, until golden and heated through. Makes 4.

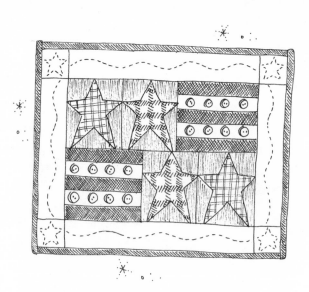

Hang up a country-style peg rack inside the back door...you'll always know where to find your umbrella, the kids' backpacks and even Spot's leash!

Come & Get It!

Tuna Pasta Primavera

Sherry Kirchheimer
La Canada, CA

*Add some chopped red pepper along with the broccoli
and carrots for added color.*

8-oz. pkg. rotini pasta,
    uncooked
2 heads broccoli, cut into
    flowerets
4 carrots, peeled and chopped
12-oz. can tuna, drained

1/2 c. mayonnaise
1/4 c. milk
1/4 c. grated Parmesan cheese
1/2 t. garlic powder
1/2 t. dried basil
1/4 t. pepper

Cook pasta according to package directions, adding broccoli and
carrots to cooking water during last 5 minutes of cooking. Drain and
return to pan. Mix remaining ingredients together and add to pasta;
toss to coat. Makes 4 to 6 servings.

If your favorite armchair is starting to look a little shabby,
spruce it up in a twinkling! Fit a chenille bedspread over the chair
and carefully tuck in around the edges...good as new!

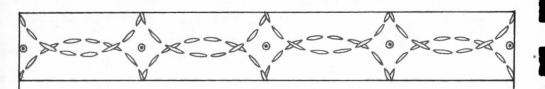

Fettuccine with Smoked Salmon

Carole Larkins
Elmendorf AFB, AK

*I like to serve this spooned into a serving bowl
ringed with fresh lettuce leaves.*

8-oz. pkg. fettuccine, uncooked
1 lb. asparagus, cut into
   1/2-inch pieces
1 c. whipping cream
2 T. fresh dill, chopped

1 T. prepared horseradish
6-oz. pkg. smoked salmon,
   cut into 1/2-inch pieces
salt and pepper to taste

Cook pasta according to package directions; add asparagus for last
3 minutes of cooking time. Drain and set aside. Warm cream, dill and
horseradish in a skillet over low heat until hot, about one minute;
add pasta mixture, tossing to mix. Gently toss in salmon; add salt and
pepper to taste. Serves 4 to 6.

If you have young children who like to color lots & lots of
pictures for you, share their creativity with family members by
using colored pages as wrapping paper.

HappY Endings

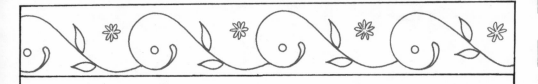

Coconut Cream Pie

Nancy Likens
Wooster, OH

Mmm...it's just as good as we remember!

2-1/2 T. cornstarch
2 c. milk, divided
1 c. sugar
1/2 t. salt
1/2 c. plus 2 to 3 T. sweetened
　　flaked coconut, divided

2 pasteurized egg whites,
　　stiffly beaten
1 t. vanilla extract
9-inch pie crust, baked

Dissolve cornstarch in 1/2 cup milk; set aside. Combine remaining milk, sugar and salt in a double boiler; bring to boiling. Reduce to medium-low heat; stir in cornstarch mixture and cook until thick, stirring frequently, for about 5 to 7 minutes. Remove from heat. Fold 1/2 cup coconut into beaten egg whites; add to milk mixture. Stir in vanilla. Pour into pie crust; sprinkle with remaining coconut. Serves 6 to 8.

A curvy wrought iron table & chair set is perfect for sharing a cup of tea with a friend. Give it new life by spraying on pastel pink or yellow paint and add comfy chair cushions...so welcoming!

Decadent Pie

Sharon Denney
Rosendale, MO

It's the best pecan pie ever...with chocolate and coconut too!

3/4 c. brown sugar, packed
3/4 c. corn syrup
4 1-oz. sqs. semi-sweet
   baking chocolate
6 T. margarine
3 eggs
1 c. chopped pecans

1-1/3 c. sweetened
   flaked coconut
9-inch pie crust
Optional: 1 T. bourbon
Garnish: 1-1/4 c. whipped
   topping, chocolate shavings

Combine brown sugar and corn syrup in a large microwave-safe bowl;
microwave on high for 4 minutes, or until boiling. Add chocolate and
margarine; stir until chocolate is completely melted. Cool slightly.
Add eggs one at a time, beating well after each addition. Stir in pecans
and coconut. Pour into unbaked pie crust. Bake at 350 degrees for
one hour, or until a knife tip inserted in center comes out clean. Cool
on wire rack. Stir bourbon into whipped topping, if desired. Garnish
cooled pie with dollops of whipped cream and chocolate shavings.
Serves 6 to 8.

*Dress up plain pillar candles in an instant...press in fancy brass
upholstery tacks or map pins to form spirals, stars, stripes or
other simple patterns.*

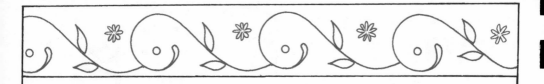

Peanut Butter Pie

Judy Adams
Wooster, OH

A yummy treat from Amish country.

2/3 c. chunky peanut butter
1/2 c. cream cheese, softened
3-1/2 oz. pkg. instant vanilla
   pudding mix

1 c. milk
1/3 c. brown sugar, packed
9-inch pie crust, baked

Blend peanut butter and cream cheese in a large bowl. Beat pudding mix into peanut butter mixture with an electric mixer on low speed, gradually adding milk. Add brown sugar and mix well; pour into crust. Freeze until firm. Thaw 30 to 45 minutes before serving if pie has been frozen more than 2 hours. Serves 6 to 8.

A country-style mailbox is just the right shape to become a
breadbox for the kitchen counter. Paint it and stencil
"Our Daily Bread" on the side.

Happy ★ Endings

Grandmother Henry's Molasses Pie

Kim Henry
South Park, PA

My family eats up this sweet pie so quickly,
I always have to make 2!

1 c. all-purpose flour
1/3 c. sugar
1/4 t. salt
1 T. shortening

1/3 c. molasses
1/3 t. baking soda
1/3 c. water
8-inch pie crust

Mix together flour, sugar, salt and shortening until crumbly; set aside 1/4 cup for topping. In a separate bowl, combine molasses and baking soda. Stir well, then add water; combine with flour mixture. Mix well; pour into unbaked pie crust. Sprinkle top with reserved topping. Bake at 425 degrees for 20 to 35 minutes, or until firm in center. If not firm after 35 minutes, turn oven down to 400 degrees; continue baking an additional several minutes until firm. Serves 4 to 6.

The most adorable illustrations can be found in vintage books of nursery rhymes. Make photocopies of your favorites, clip out and découpage onto children's furniture...headboard, dresser and even across the top of a little rocking chair.

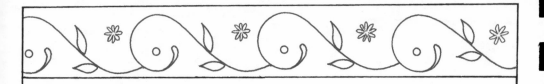

Rhubarb Chess Pie

Barb Hansen
Buffalo City, WI

*A real old-fashioned pie...you'll find rhubarb
at your local farmers' market.*

2 c. rhubarb, cut in
    1/2-inch slices
8-inch pie crust
1-1/4 c. sugar
1/4 c. butter, softened
3 eggs

1 T. cider vinegar
1 t. vanilla extract
Optional: 2 to 3 drops
    red food coloring
Garnish: cinnamon

Place rhubarb in unbaked pie crust; set aside. In a medium bowl, combine sugar and butter and set aside. Beat eggs in a small bowl; add vinegar and vanilla. Add egg mixture to sugar mixture; mix well. Tint with food coloring, if desired. Pour over rhubarb; sprinkle cinnamon over top. Bake at 350 degrees for 50 to 60 minutes, or until golden and puffed slightly. Serves 6 to 8.

Don't pass up discarded window frames at yard sales. Carefully push out any glass with gloved hands and paint, or leave unpainted for a rustic look. Place small mirrors in the openings or even give a blank corner a new view by mounting a scenic poster behind the frame.

Strawberry-Cream Cheese Pie

Lori Simmons
Princeville, IL

I love this combination of strawberries and cream cheese...a great pie for summer picnics!

10-oz. pkg. frozen strawberries
   in syrup
2 8-oz. pkgs. cream cheese,
   softened
1/4 c. sugar

2 c. frozen whipped topping,
   thawed
9-inch chocolate graham
   cracker crust

Thaw and drain strawberries, reserving 1/4 cup syrup. Beat together cream cheese, strawberries, reserved syrup and sugar. Fold in whipped topping. Pour filling into graham cracker crust and refrigerate. Serves 6 to 8.

A vintage lace tablecloth is quickly turned into the prettiest window topper...simply attach clip-on curtain rings.

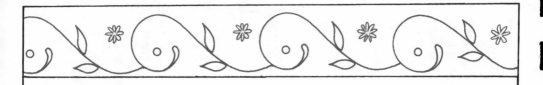

Crustless Apple Pie

Mona Hands
Ontario, Canada

*Jonagold, Rome and Golden Delicious apples are
some good choices for pie baking.*

5 apples, cored, peeled
   and sliced
1 t. cinnamon
1 c. plus 1 T. sugar, divided

3/4 c. margarine, melted
1 c. all-purpose flour
1 egg, beaten

Place apples in a greased 2-quart casserole dish; sprinkle with
cinnamon and one tablespoon sugar. Mix remaining ingredients;
spread over apples. Bake at 350 degrees for 50 to 60 minutes.
Serves 6 to 8.

For the sweetest kitchen border, trace around
favorite cookie cutters. Paint the outlines with a small brush
and acrylic craft paint.

HaPPY Endings

Cherry Crumb Pie

Mary Jo Wallis
Independence, KS

We cannot tell a lie...this is a luscious pie!

1 T. cornstarch
1 T. cold water
21-oz. can cherry pie filling
9-inch graham cracker crust
1/3 c. all-purpose flour

1/3 c. quick-cooking oats,
  uncooked
2 T. sugar
2 T. brown sugar, packed
3 T. butter

Mix cornstarch and water until smooth; stir in pie filling. Pour into pie crust and set aside. In a separate bowl, combine flour, oats and sugars; cut in butter. Sprinkle over filling. Bake at 375 degrees for 35 to 40 minutes, until crust is golden and filling is bubbly. Cool on a wire rack; refrigerate until chilled. Serves 6 to 8.

A merry heart doeth good like a medicine.

−Proverbs 17:22

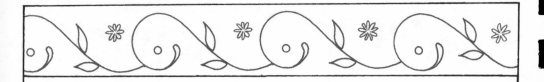

Lemonade Pie

Staci Meyers
Cocoa, FL

*Make any flavor you like by substituting a different flavor of
frozen fruit drink concentrate...try orange or raspberry.*

1 qt. vanilla ice cream, softened   9-inch graham cracker crust
6-oz. can frozen lemonade
   concentrate, softened

Combine ice cream and lemonade concentrate; mix well. Spoon into
crust and freeze for at least 4 hours, or until firm. Let stand at room
temperature for a few minutes before serving. Serves 6 to 8.

Give plain-Jane glass hurricane
shades a new look. Cut dots or
hearts from self-adhesive clear
plastic and arrange them over the
surface of the shade, then spray
with glass frosting paint. Let dry,
then peel off plastic shapes. Great
on clear glass vases and cake
covers too!

Key Lime Pie

Michelle Elliott
Loveland, CO

A classic!

1-1/2 c. vanilla wafers, crushed
1/4 c. butter, melted
8-oz. pkg. cream cheese,
   softened
14-oz. can sweetened
   condensed milk

1/3 c. lime juice
1 T. lime zest
2 to 3 drops green food coloring
8-oz. container frozen
   whipped topping, thawed

Mix wafer crumbs with butter; pat into a 9" pie plate. Bake at
350 degrees for 10 minutes; cool. Blend together cream cheese and
condensed milk. Add lime juice, lime zest and green coloring. Fold in
whipped topping; pour into crust and chill for 30 minutes. Serves 6.

Grandma's kitchen
stepstool...so handy
for little ones to perch on.
Freshen it up with a new coat of
paint and clippings from seed
packets découpaged on.

Chocolate Chip Party Cake

Lise Godfrey
Eglin AFB, FL

Your party guests will be impressed...only you know how easy it is!

18-1/4 oz. pkg. yellow cake mix
2 3-1/2 oz. pkgs. instant
   chocolate pudding mix
4 eggs
1 c. oil

1-1/2 c. water
12-oz. pkg. semi-sweet
   chocolate chips
Garnish: powdered sugar

Stir together first 5 ingredients in a mixing bowl; add chocolate chips.
Pour into a greased Bundt® pan. Bake at 350 degrees for 45 minutes.
Let cool in pan for 10 minutes; turn out of pan. When completely cool,
sprinkle with powdered sugar. Serves 10 to 12.

A touch of whimsy...use Mom's old cow-shaped milk pitcher to
top desserts with cream or chocolate sauce.

Coal Miners' Cake

Susie Leonard
Port Royal, PA

Try different combinations of cake mix and pie filling...spice cake with apple pie filling is good too.

18-1/4 oz. pkg. devil's food
   cake mix
21-oz. can cherry pie filling

2 eggs
1 t. vanilla extract

Combine all ingredients; mix well. Pour into a lightly greased 13"x9" baking pan. Bake at 350 degrees for 30 to 35 minutes. While cake is still hot, spread with Chocolate-Pecan Topping. Serves 8 to 10.

Chocolate-Pecan Topping:

1/2 c. butter
1/4 c. evaporated milk
1 c. sugar

6-oz. pkg. semi-sweet
   chocolate chips
1/2 c. chopped pecans

Combine first 3 ingredients in a saucepan. Bring to a slow boil over low heat; boil for one minute. Add chocolate chips and nuts; stir until chocolate melts.

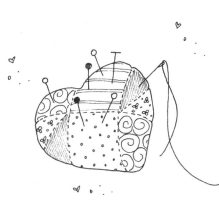

Worn-out quilts can enjoy new life when turned into table toppers or throw pillows. Even the smallest scraps can be turned into a tiny pincushion or an herb-filled sleep pillow...sweet and simple!

World's Best Carrot Cake

Shannon Buland
Brigham City, UT

Stir in some plump golden raisins for extra sweetness.

2 c. sugar
2 c. all-purpose flour
1 t. salt
2 t. cinnamon

2 t. baking soda
5 eggs
1-1/2 c. oil
2 c. carrots, peeled and grated

Mix sugar, flour, salt, cinnamon and baking soda in a medium bowl; set aside. Beat eggs and oil together in another bowl; add to dry ingredients. Stir carrots into batter; pour into a greased 13"x9" baking pan. Bake at 350 degrees for 30 to 35 minutes. Let cool; spread Cream Cheese-Walnut Icing on top. Serves 8 to 10.

Cream Cheese-Walnut Icing:

8-oz. pkg. cream cheese,
   softened
1 to 2 T. butter

16-oz. pkg. powdered sugar
1 t. vanilla extract
1 c. chopped walnuts

Blend together cream cheese and butter; add powdered sugar and vanilla. Mix until smooth and creamy; stir in nuts.

Did you find some vintage curtains in a fun print at a yard sale, but don't need new curtains? Turn them quickly into big throw pillows for the sofa or make a sturdy tote bag for future sales.

Grandma's Oatmeal Cake

Karen Stroup
East Berlin, PA

I cherish this recipe from my grandmother's recipe box.

2-1/2 c. boiling water
1-1/2 c. quick-cooking oats,
   uncooked
3/4 c. shortening
1-1/2 c. sugar
1-1/2 c. brown sugar, packed

3 eggs, beaten
1-1/2 t. baking soda
1-1/2 t. salt
1-1/2 t. cinnamon
2-1/4 c. all-purpose flour
3/4 c. chopped pecans

Pour boiling water over oats in a heat-proof bowl; let stand for
5 minutes. Blend together shortening, sugars and eggs in another
bowl. Add oat mixture and stir; add baking soda, salt, cinnamon and
flour. Stir well and add pecans. Pour into a greased 13"x9" baking
pan. Bake at 350 degrees for 50 to 55 minutes. Check center for
doneness with a toothpick. Frost with MeMa's Icing. Serves 8 to 10.

MeMa's Icing:

1 c. milk
6 T. all-purpose flour
3/4 c. shortening

1 c. sugar
1/8 to 1/4 t. vanilla extract
1/8 t. salt

Mix milk and flour in a small saucepan. Cook over medium heat
until a stiff ball of dough forms. Let cool completely. Beat shortening
and sugar in a small bowl until very light and fluffy. Add cooled
milk mixture; beat well. Add vanilla to taste and salt.

A pottery pitcher makes
handy storage for
wooden spoons, spatulas
and other cooking tools.

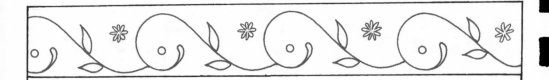

Apple Cake

Marilyn Beil
Williamsville, NY

This recipe is from my grandmother…she was a wonderful cook!

4 c. apples, cored, peeled
   and chopped
2 c. sugar
2 eggs, beaten
1/2 c. oil
2 t. vanilla extract

2 c. all-purpose flour
2 t. baking soda
1 t. salt
2 t. cinnamon
Optional: 1 c. chopped nuts

Mix together apples and sugar in a large bowl; let stand for 5 minutes. Stir together eggs, oil and vanilla; add to apple mixture. Mix together remaining ingredients and add to apple mixture. Pour into a greased 13"x9" baking pan; bake at 350 degrees for 50 minutes. Makes 10 to 12 servings.

A tin school lunchbox is perfect for storing favorite recipes.

HaPPY Endings

Wacky Cake

Linda Nichols
Steubenville, OH

It only takes 10 minutes to mix up this moist chocolate cake in the pan it's baked in...good plain or with a scoop of vanilla ice cream!

1-1/2 c. all-purpose flour
1 c. sugar
1/4 c. baking cocoa
1 t. baking powder
1 t. baking soda

1/4 t. salt
1 c. water
1/3 c. oil
1/4 c. white vinegar
1 t. vanilla extract

Sift together flour, sugar, cocoa, baking powder, baking soda and salt into an ungreased 8"x8" baking pan. Make a well in the center and pour in remaining ingredients; mix until well blended. Bake at 350 degrees for 25 to 30 minutes, or until a toothpick inserted in the center tests done. Serves 6 to 8.

Top hot-from-the-oven chocolate cupcakes with a dollop of marshmallow creme...yummy!

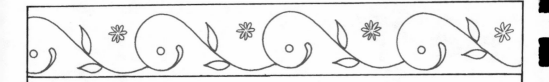

Fresh Blueberry Cake

Dianna Likens
Gooseberry Patch

Try this cake warm for breakfast too.

1/2 c. margarine, softened
2 c. sugar
2 eggs
3-1/4 c. all-purpose flour
1 t. cream of tartar
1/2 t. baking soda

1/8 t. salt
1 c. milk
2 to 4 c. blueberries
Garnish: melted butter,
   cinnamon-sugar

Blend together margarine, sugar and eggs; set aside. In a separate bowl, blend together flour, cream of tartar, baking soda and salt. Add flour mixture to margarine mixture alternately with milk. Fold in blueberries carefully. Spread into a greased and floured 2-quart casserole dish; bake at 350 degrees for 40 minutes. Brush top with butter while hot and sprinkle with cinnamon-sugar. Serves 16 to 20.

Show off a stack of special dessert plates under the glass
dome of a cake stand.

Ladyfingers Layer Cake

Mary Patenaude
Griswold, CT

A scrumptious, cool no-bake dessert.

1 c. butter, softened
2 c. powdered sugar
4 pasteurized eggs
13-1/2 oz. can crushed
    pineapple, drained

1 c. chopped nuts
2 doz. ladyfingers, split and
    divided
Garnish: frozen whipped
    topping, thawed

Blend butter and sugar in a large bowl; beat in eggs one at a time. Add pineapple and nuts; mix well. Line a 9"x5" loaf pan with wax paper. Arrange a layer of split ladyfingers in bottom of pan, filling in any spaces with broken pieces. Top with a layer of pineapple mixture. Continue layering until pan is full, ending with a layer of ladyfingers. Cover and chill for 6 to 8 hours, or overnight. Unmold and frost with whipped topping. Serves 4 to 6.

A big popcorn gift tin is easily turned into a useful
wastebasket...spray with craft paint and découpage with
cut-outs from gardening catalogs or snippets from travel
brochures. Turn over the tin's lid and it becomes
a handy serving tray.

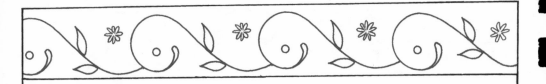

Hootenanny Cake

Kimberly Danber
Huber Heights, OH

My grandmother gave me this recipe...every time I bake it,
I think of her. It's wonderful served warm from the oven,
topped with vanilla ice cream.

18-1/4 oz. pkg. yellow cake mix
3-1/2 oz. pkg. instant
   coconut pudding mix
1/2 t. baking powder
1 c. water
4 eggs, beaten

1/2 c. oil
1 t. vanilla extract
1 c. chopped pecans
4 t. sugar
2 t. cinnamon

Mix together cake mix, pudding mix, baking powder, water, eggs, oil and vanilla; set aside. Blend together pecans, sugar and cinnamon. Place one-third of nut mixture in the bottom of a lightly greased tube pan. Top with half the cake batter. Place another one-third of nut mixture on top of cake batter, then pour remaining cake batter into pan. Top with remaining nut mixture. Bake at 350 degrees for 50 minutes to one hour. Makes 8 to 10 servings.

Big, colorful ice cubes for a party punch bowl...arrange thin slices of citrus or kiwi in muffin tins, fill with water and freeze.

Texas Tornado Cake

Joyce Roebuck
Jacksonville, TX

*This cake really looks like a tornado has hit it, but it tastes
so good that people ask me for the recipe all the time.*

1-1/2 c. sweetened flaked
   coconut
1-1/2 c. chopped pecans
18-1/4 oz. pkg. German
   chocolate cake mix
3 eggs, beaten
1-1/4 c. water

1/4 c. oil
8-oz. pkg. cream cheese,
   softened
1/2 c. butter
16-oz. pkg. powdered sugar
Optional: vanilla frosting

Sprinkle coconut and pecans into a greased, wax paper-lined
13"x9" baking pan; set aside. Stir together cake mix, eggs, water
and oil. Spoon over coconut mixture; set aside. Combine cream cheese
and butter in a saucepan over low heat; heat until butter melts. Stir in
powdered sugar; spoon over cake mixture. Bake at 350 degrees for
40 to 45 minutes; coconut and pecans will rise to the top. Let cool in
pan on a wire rack for for 10 minutes; invert onto a serving plate and
remove wax paper. If desired, frost with vanilla frosting. Serves 16.

Sparkly fairy lights for the garden...wrap tiny glass jars with
craft wire to form hangers and add some colored glass beads.
Tuck in votive candles and hang from low branches.

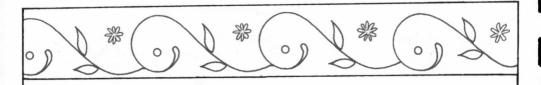

Cranberry-Orange Dream

Kimberly Boyce
Murrieta, CA

*The layers are so pretty that you'll want to show them off
in a clear glass serving bowl.*

3 3-oz. pkgs. cranberry
    gelatin mix
2-1/2 c. boiling water
2-3/4 c. cold water
15-oz. can mandarin oranges,
    drained

1/2 c. cream cheese, softened
2 T. sugar
2 8-oz. containers frozen
    whipped topping, thawed
    and divided
Optional: orange zest curls

In a medium bowl, dissolve gelatin in boiling water. Stir in cold water
and refrigerate for one hour, until slightly thickened. Gently stir in
oranges and set aside. In a separate medium bowl, beat cream cheese
and sugar with a wire whisk until well blended. Gently stir in one
container whipped topping. Spoon into a large serving bowl, spreading
evenly. Cover with gelatin mixture. Refrigerate for 4 hours or
overnight. Garnish with dollops of remaining whipped topping and a
sprinkle of orange zest, if desired. Serves 14 to 16.

Invite your favorite child
to tea. Set out a childhood
tea set along with some
tiny cookies, mini muffins
and of course pink
lemonade "tea"...so sweet!

Peach Bavarian

Kristine McLean
Bend, OR

Light, fluffy and not too sweet...a perfect ending to a hearty meal.

2 3-oz. pkgs. peach gelatin mix
1/2 c. sugar
2 c. boiling water
16-oz. can sliced peaches,
    drained, chopped and
    2/3 c. juice reserved

1 t. almond extract
8-oz. container frozen whipped
    topping, thawed
Optional: sliced peaches

In a bowl, dissolve gelatin and sugar in boiling water. Stir in reserved peach juice. Chill until slightly thickened. Stir extract into whipped topping; gently fold into gelatin mixture. Fold in peaches; pour into a greased 6-cup mold. Chill overnight. Unmold and garnish with additional sliced peaches, if desired. Serves 8 to 10.

A collection of gleaming copper molds makes a beautiful, useful display on a kitchen wall. Be sure to hang them where they'll glitter in the sunshine.

Chocolate Eclair Dessert

Maggie Malinowski
Culver City, CA

You won't believe how delicious this is...yet so easy!

14-1/2 oz. pkg. graham crackers
2 3-1/2 oz. pkgs. instant
   vanilla pudding mix

3 c. milk
8-oz. container frozen
   whipped topping, thawed

Line the bottom of a greased 13"x9" baking pan with graham crackers; set aside. Mix pudding mix with milk until thickened; fold in whipped topping. Pour half of pudding mixture over crackers; top with another layer of crackers. Pour remaining pudding mixture on top; arrange remaining crackers on top. Spread with Chocolate Frosting; chill for 24 hours before serving. Serves 12.

Chocolate Frosting:

1-1/2 c. powdered sugar
2 T. margarine, softened
2 T. corn syrup

2 1-oz. sqs. unsweetened
   baking chocolate, melted
3 T. milk

Mix all ingredients together until smooth.

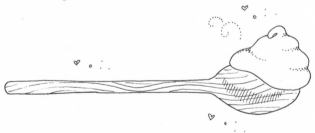

Turn a bookcase into a dollhouse...a perfect place for children to imagine. Cut lengths of wood to fit between shelves and tack in to form "rooms", then decorate with paint and wallpaper samples.

Peanutty Torte

Jolayne Robbins
De Pere, WI

Crush the graham crackers and peanuts easily...seal them in
large plastic zipping bags and roll over the bags with a rolling pin.

2 c. graham crackers, crushed
1/2 c. butter, melted
2/3 c. Spanish peanuts, crushed
   and divided
2 8-oz. pkgs. cream cheese,
   softened
1/3 c. creamy peanut butter

1 c. powdered sugar
12-oz. container frozen whipped
   topping, thawed and divided
2 3-1/2 oz. pkgs. instant
   chocolate pudding mix
3 c. milk

Combine graham crackers, butter and 1/3 cup peanuts; press into an
ungreased 13"x9" baking pan. Bake for 10 minutes at 350 degrees.
Cool slightly. Combine cream cheese, peanut butter and powdered
sugar; fold in 2 cups whipped topping. Pour over cooled crust.
Combine pudding mix and milk; spread over first layer. Spread
remaining whipped topping over top and sprinkle with remaining
peanuts. Keep refrigerated. Makes 8 to 10 servings.

It's a fact...a big bouquet
of fresh flowers
is always a welcome gift!
Keep flowers fresh a few
days longer by adding a
sugar cube and a spoonful
of bleach to the water in
the vase.

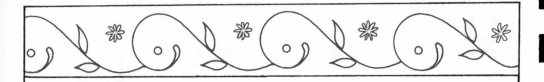

Apple Kuchen

Regina Elledge
Collierville, TN

This recipe is a long-time tradition in my husband's family...one of his brothers always requests this for his birthday.

18-1/4 oz. pkg. yellow cake mix
1/2 c. margarine, softened
1/2 c. sweetened flaked coconut
20-oz. can sliced apples, drained

1/2 c. sugar
1 t. cinnamon
16-oz. container sour cream
1 egg, beaten

Combine cake mix, margarine and coconut and press into a lightly greased 13"x9" baking pan. Bake at 350 degrees for 10 minutes. Arrange apple slices in baked crust. Mix sugar and cinnamon; sprinkle over apples. Mix sour cream and egg; spread over all. Return to oven and bake for an additional 25 minutes. Serves 12.

Small candles floating in water-filled glass goblets add sparkle to the dinner table...quick & easy.

Creamy Banana Pudding

Elizabeth Cox
Lewisville, TX

Everyone's childhood comfort food...you never outgrow it!

5-1/4 oz. pkg. instant vanilla
   pudding mix
8-oz. container frozen whipped
   topping, thawed
8-oz. pkg. cream cheese,
   softened

1 t. vanilla extract
16-oz. pkg. vanilla wafers,
   crushed
4 bananas, sliced
Optional: whipped topping,
   vanilla wafer crumbs

Prepare pudding mix in a large bowl as directed; chill. Add whipped topping, cream cheese and vanilla to pudding. Mix until thick and well blended. In a 2-quart casserole dish, layer crushed vanilla wafers, banana slices and pudding mixture. Top with additional whipped topping and crushed vanilla wafers, if desired. Chill before serving. Serves 8 to 10.

It takes a heap o' livin' in a house to make it home.
–Edgar A. Guest

Too-Easy Cherry Cobbler

Caitlin Welch
Selma, AL

I am happy to share this scrumptious southern recipe with you!

2 21-oz. cans cherry pie filling
15-oz. can dark sweet cherries,
   drained
1/4 c. all-purpose flour, divided
1/2 t. almond extract
5 slices white bread,
   crusts trimmed

1-1/4 c. sugar
1/2 c. butter, melted
1 egg, beaten
1-1/2 t. lemon zest

Stir together pie filling, cherries, 2 tablespoons flour and extract.
Place in a lightly greased 8"x8" baking pan. Cut each slice of bread
into 5 strips; arrange strips over fruit mixture. In a medium bowl,
stir together remaining flour, sugar, butter, egg and lemon zest.
Drizzle over bread strips. Bake at 350 degrees for 35 to 45 minutes,
or until golden and bubbly. Serves 4 to 6.

Stack up vintage tin
or wicker picnic baskets in a
corner of the kitchen...instant
nostalgia plus storage for
cookbooks, cookie cutters and
other items.

Easy Slow-Cooker Fruit Dessert

Karla Ihrke
Owatonna, MN

This recipe is oh-so-easy and very good with vanilla ice cream.

21-oz. can cherry or apple
   pie filling
18-oz. pkg. yellow cake mix

1/2 c. butter, melted
Optional: 1/3 c. chopped walnuts

Pour pie filling into a slow cooker; set aside. Combine cake mix and butter; mix until crumbly. Sprinkle over pie filling; top with walnuts, if using. Cover and cook on low setting for 2 to 3 hours. Serve warm. Makes 8 to 10 servings.

Keep a big bowl filled with fresh fruit in the kitchen, handy for snacking...try shiny apples and pears in summer, oranges and kiwi fruit in winter.

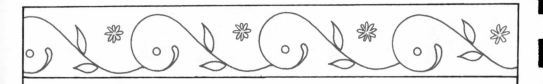

Pistachio Surprise

Cindy Tenuta
Racine, WI

Add a drop or 2 of green food coloring for pistachio-green color.

1-1/2 c. all-purpose flour
1/2 c. margarine
1/2 c. chopped walnuts
8-oz. pkg. cream cheese,
   softened
1 c. powdered sugar

8-oz. container frozen whipped
   topping, thawed and divided
2 3-1/2 oz. pkgs. instant
   pistachio pudding mix
3 c. milk
Optional: chopped walnuts

Mix flour, margarine and walnuts together. Press into a greased
13"x9" baking pan. Bake at 350 degrees for 18 minutes; cool.
Combine cream cheese, powdered sugar and half of whipped topping.
Whip together until smooth; spread on cooled crust. Mix together
pudding mix, milk and remaining whipped topping until smooth.
Spread over cream cheese mixture. Sprinkle with additional walnuts,
if desired. Chill for several hours before serving. Serves 12 to 16.

Fill pitchers to overflowing with sunflowers, zinnias or daisies
for a bright summertime welcome.

HaPPY · Endings

Strawberry Tiffany Torte

Cheryl McCullough
Botkins, OH

I love this recipe because it reminds me of summer
and the first mouthwatering ripe strawberries!

3 c. vanilla wafers, crushed
1/2 c. shortening, melted
4 c. milk, divided
2 8-oz. pkgs. cream cheese,
   softened

2 3-3/4 oz. pkgs. instant
   vanilla pudding mix
1 qt. strawberries, sliced
8-oz. container frozen whipped
   topping, thawed

Combine vanilla wafer crumbs and shortening; set aside one cup
of mixture for topping. Press remaining mixture into the bottom of a
greased 13"x9" baking pan. Gradually add one cup milk to cream
cheese; mix until well blended. Add pudding mix and remaining milk.
Beat slowly for one minute; pour over crust. Refrigerate to set.
Cover set pudding mixture with strawberries. Top with whipped
topping and reserved crumb mixture. Chill several hours or overnight.
Serves 8 to 10.

Ice cream will stay fresh and tasty
every time the carton is opened...press a piece of wax paper
over the surface before reclosing.

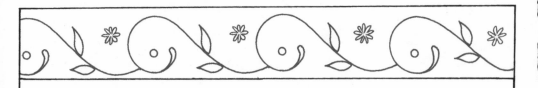

Best-Ever Brownies

Jen Burnham
Delaware, OH

*These delicious brownies are as easy as a boxed mix
and twice as tasty.*

12-oz. pkg. semi-sweet
   chocolate chips, divided
1/4 c. butter
3/4 c. sugar
2 eggs, beaten

1 c. all-purpose flour
1/8 t. salt
1 t. vanilla extract
1/2 c. plus 2 T. chopped
   walnuts, divided

Combine one cup chocolate chips and butter in a microwave-safe medium bowl. Microwave on high setting for one minute. Stir until smooth; whisk in sugar and eggs. Stir in flour and salt until smooth. Fold in vanilla and 1/2 cup walnuts. Transfer to a greased 8"x8" glass baking pan. Bake at 350 degrees for 23 to 25 minutes. Sprinkle remaining chocolate chips over top in an even layer; bake an additional 2 minutes. Remove from oven and gently spread melted chips until smooth to form a frosting. Top with remaining nuts. Chill for 20 minutes to firm chocolate; cut into squares. Makes 16.

Create a giant cookie pizza as a special birthday treat. Press refrigerated sugar cookie dough onto an ungreased pizza pan and bake as directed. When cool, spread with frosting...decorate with candy toppings like fruit leather, licorice strings and candy-coated chocolates. Fun!

Grace's No-Bake Fudge Squares

Lisa Hains
Tipp City, OH

*This recipe was shared by Grace, a dear friend of my grandmother.
These are quick to make and oh-so yummy! They freeze well for
unexpected company...but you may have to hide them!*

1/2 c. brown sugar, packed
1 egg, beaten
1/2 c. butter

2 c. graham cracker crumbs
1/2 c. sweetened flaked coconut
1/2 c. chopped nuts

Combine brown sugar, egg and butter in a saucepan over low heat;
bring to a boil and cook for one minute. Remove from heat and
quickly stir in cracker crumbs, coconut and nuts. Immediately press
into a greased 8"x8" baking pan. Chill until firm. Frost with Buttery
Cocoa Frosting; chill again until firm. Cut into squares. Serves 16.

Buttery Cocoa Frosting:

1/4 c. butter
3 T. water
1/2 t. vanilla extract

3 T. baking cocoa
1 to 2 c. powdered sugar

Melt butter in a saucepan over low heat. Stir in water, vanilla, cocoa
and enough powdered sugar to make a spreading consistency.

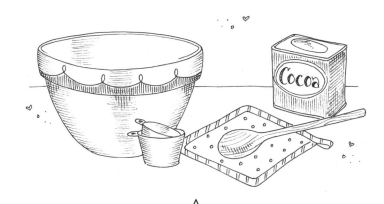

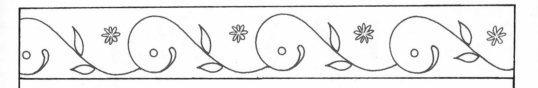

Apricot Squares

Cathy Smith
Branchville, NJ

Delightful with a cup of almond tea.

2/3 c. dried apricots
1/2 c. butter, softened
1/4 c. sugar
1-1/3 c. all-purpose flour,
    divided
1 c. brown sugar, packed

2 eggs
1/2 c. chopped walnuts
1/2 t. baking powder
1/2 t. vanilla extract
1/4 t. salt

Cover apricots with water in a one-quart saucepan. Cook, covered, over low heat for 15 minutes. Drain and chop; set aside. Combine butter, sugar and one cup flour in a large bowl; mix with an electric mixer on medium speed until crumbly. Pat into a greased 8"x8" baking pan. Bake at 350 degrees for 25 minutes, until golden. In another bowl, mix apricots, remaining flour and brown sugar; add remaining ingredients. Pour over baked layer and bake for an additional 25 minutes. Cool in pan and cut into squares. Makes 6 to 8 servings.

There's nothing like a spicy scent in the air to make a house feel like home! Pop a few cinnamon sticks and whole cloves into a small saucepan of water and keep it simmering...that fresh-baked aroma will fill the house!

Blueberry-Lemon Nut Bars

Linda Patten
Lake Zurich, IL

*I've made these bars with pecans, walnuts and
even macadamia nuts. They're always scrumptious!*

2 c. plus 3 T. all-purpose
   flour, divided
3/4 c. butter, softened
1/2 c. chopped nuts
1/2 c. powdered sugar
2 T. lemon zest, divided

4 eggs, beaten
2 c. sugar
1/4 c. lemon juice
1/2 t. baking powder
1-1/2 c. blueberries

Combine 2 cups flour, butter, nuts, powdered sugar and one
tablespoon lemon zest in a large bowl; mix well. Pat evenly into the
bottom of a lightly greased 13"x9" baking pan. Bake at 350 degrees
for 20 to 25 minutes, until golden; set aside. Combine eggs, sugar,
lemon juice, remaining zest, remaining flour and baking powder in a
bowl; pour over crust. Sprinkle evenly with blueberries; bake an
additional 15 to 20 minutes, until top is golden. Cool and cut into
squares. Makes 2 dozen.

Use new plastic sand pails to serve snacks or ice at parties...use
a sand shovel as a server!

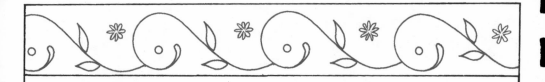

Great-Grandma's Nut Cups

Debi Benson
Mount Pleasant, SC

These tiny pecan tarts are perfect for a dessert tray.

1 lb. pecans, finely chopped
1-1/2 c. plus 2 T. sugar, divided
1 c. margarine, softened
   and divided
1 egg, beaten

1 c. milk
2 3-oz. pkgs. cream cheese,
   softened
2-2/3 c. all-purpose flour
1/8 t. salt

Blend together pecans, 1-1/2 cups sugar, 1/2 cup margarine, egg and milk in a saucepan. Cook over medium heat until mixture comes to a slow boil. Remove from heat; set aside. In a large bowl, combine remaining margarine, cream cheese, remaining sugar, flour and salt; press mixture into ungreased mini muffin cups. Fill with pecan mixture. Bake at 350 degrees for 25 to 30 minutes. Turn tins upside-down and let cool. Makes 4 dozen.

Sunny daisies tucked into pint-size milk bottles in a wire bottle carrier...what could be more delightful?

Cream Cheese Tarts

Judy Harris
Dugway, UT

These are delectable...very pretty for special occasions.

3/4 c. sugar
2 8-oz. pkgs. cream cheese,
    softened
1 T. lemon juice

2 eggs, beaten
20 to 22 vanilla wafers
21-oz. can cherry or blueberry
    pie filling

Blend sugar and cream cheese together in a large bowl; add lemon juice and eggs. Blend until smooth; set aside. Line muffin cups with paper liners. Place one wafer in each cup; fill each 1/2 full with cream cheese mixture. Bake at 325 degrees for 25 minutes; cool. Top each tart with a dollop of pie filling. Makes 20 to 22 tarts.

Welcome new neighbors with a basket of homemade cookies...slip in a map of the neighborhood with all of your favorite spots marked with shiny stars.

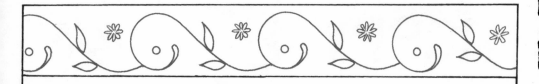

Judy's No-Bake Cookies

Pamela Canfield
Dearborn, MI

My mother-in-law, Judy, was a school cook for many years. The students just loved these cookies and so did her 7 children!

4 c. sugar
1 c. butter
1/2 c. baking cocoa
1 c. milk

1-1/2 c. creamy peanut butter
6 c. quick-cooking oats,
  uncooked
1 t. vanilla extract

Combine sugar, butter, cocoa and milk in a saucepan. Bring to a boil over medium heat; boil for 2 minutes. Remove from heat; stir in peanut butter until melted. Mix in oats and vanilla; stir until coated with cocoa mixture. Drop by teaspoonfuls onto wax paper; let cool. Makes about 8 dozen.

Dress a teddy bear in outgrown baby clothes and pose in a child-size chair...so sweet!

Cocoa-Cherry Macaroons

Charity Meyer
Lewisberry, PA

Tuck a dozen of these delights into a candy box for a sweet gift.

6 c. sweetened flaked coconut
14-oz. can sweetened
   condensed milk
1 t. vanilla extract

1 c. semi-sweet mini
   chocolate chips
1/2 c. maraschino cherries,
   drained and chopped

Combine coconut, condensed milk and vanilla in a large bowl; mix until coconut is well coated. Stir in chocolate chips and cherries. Drop by heaping teaspoonfuls 2 inches apart on a parchment paper-lined baking sheet. Bake at 350 degrees for 7 to 8 minutes. Makes 4 dozen.

Don't discard the red juice from jars of maraschino cherries.
Stir into lemonade for a sweet pink treat!

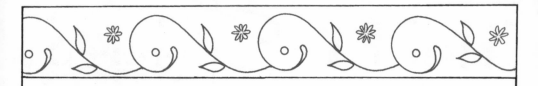

Mexican Wedding Cakes

Lisa Atkinson
Johnstown, OH

We like to roll the warm cookies in powdered sugar.

1 c. butter, softened
1/4 c. sugar
1 t. vanilla extract

2 c. all-purpose flour
1/2 c. chopped walnuts

Blend butter, sugar and vanilla together; add flour and walnuts. Shape into one-inch balls; place on greased baking sheets. Bake at 325 degrees for 18 to 20 minutes. Makes 3 dozen.

A chocolate lover's delight...so easy! Fill a mini slow cooker with chips or chunks of chocolate and heat on low until melted. Stir, then dip in whole strawberries, cookies, you name it. Yummy!

Irresistible Caramel Bars

Linda Gable
Dublin, OH

So tempting...bet you can't eat just one!

3/4 c. butter-flavored shortening
3 c. brown sugar, packed
3 eggs
1 T. vanilla extract

1-3/4 c. all-purpose flour
1 T. baking powder
1/2 t. salt
1 c. chopped nuts

Blend shortening and brown sugar together in a large bowl. Blend in eggs and vanilla; mix well and set aside. Sift together flour, baking powder and salt; add to shortening mixture. Stir in nuts; spread in a greased and floured 13"x9" baking pan. Bake at 350 degrees for 35 to 40 minutes. Cut into bars when cool. Makes 1-1/2 to 2 dozen.

Make a fabric liner for a basket of goodies...no sewing required! Cut an 18-inch square of homespun and pull away the threads at the edges to create fringes as long as you like.

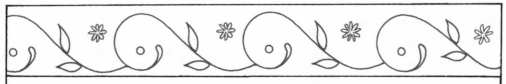

Simple Substitutions

Ingredient	Quantity	Substitutions
Baking cocoa	1/4 c.	1 oz. unsweetened chocolate, subtract 1-1/2 t. butter or oil in recipe
Baking powder	1 t.	1/4 t. baking soda plus 1/2 t. cream of tartar
Baking soda		no substitute
Beans, dried	1 lb., cooked	3 15-oz. cans beans
Broth	1 c.	1 c. boiling water plus 1 cube bouillon or 1 t. bouillon granules
Brown sugar	1 c.	1 c. sugar plus 2 T. molasses
Butter	1 c.	1 c. shortening plus 2 T. water
Buttermilk	1 c.	1 c. minus 1 T. milk plus 1 T. vinegar, let stand 5 mins.
Cake flour	1 c.	1 c. minus 2 T. all-purpose flour
Catsup	1 c.	1 c. tomato sauce plus 1/2 c. sugar and 2 t. vinegar (for cooking use)
Chocolate, semi-sweet	1 oz.	1 oz. unsweetened chocolate plus 1 t. sugar
Chocolate, unsweetened	1 oz.	3 T. baking cocoa plus 1 T. butter or oil
Cornstarch	1 T.	2 T. all-purpose flour
Egg	1 medium	1/4 c. egg substitute
Garlic	1 clove	1 t. minced garlic or 1/8 t. garlic powder
Half-and-half	1 c.	3/4 c. milk plus 1/3 c. melted butter
Herbs, fresh	1 T., chopped	1 t. dried herbs
Lemon juice	1 T.	1-1/2 t. vinegar

Ingredient	Quantity	Substitutions
Milk	1 c.	1/2 c. evaporated milk plus 1/2 c. water
Mustard, prepared	2 t.	1 t. dry mustard
Onion	1 medium	2 T. dried, chopped onion or 1-1/2 t. onion powder
Sour cream	1 c.	1 c. plain yogurt or 1 c. cottage cheese, blended smooth
Soy sauce	1 T.	1 T. Worcestershire sauce + 1 t. water
Sugar	1 c.	1-3/4 c. powdered sugar or 1 c. brown sugar, packed
Tomato sauce	1 c.	3/4 c. tomato paste plus 1/4 c. water
Vinegar	1 T.	2 T. lemon juice
Whipping cream	1 c., whipped	2 c. frozen whipped topping, thawed
Worcestershire sauce	1 T.	1 T. steak sauce
Yogurt	1 c.	1 c. cottage cheese plus 1 t. lemon juice, blended until smooth

Kitchen Measurements

A pinch = 1/8 tablespoon
3 teaspoons = 1 tablespoon
2 tablespoons = 1/8 cup
4 tablespoons = 1/4 cup
8 tablespoons = 1/2 cup
16 tablespoons = 1 cup
2 cups = 1 pint
4 cups = 1 quart
4 quarts = 1 gallon

1 fluid ounce = 2 tablespoons
4 fluid ounces = 1/2 cup
8 fluid ounces = 1 cup
16 fluid ounces = 1 pint
32 fluid ounces = 1 quart
16 ounces net weight = 1 pound

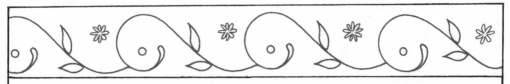

Easy Equivalents

Ingredient	Quantity	Equivalents
Bacon	1 lb.	1-1/2 c., cooked and crumbled
Beef, ground	1 lb.	2 c., cooked
Butter	1 stick	1/2 c.
Carrots	2 medium	1 c., chopped
Celery	3 stalks	1 c., chopped
Cheese, Cheddar	8-oz. package	2 c., shredded
Cheese, cream	8-oz. package	1 c.
Chicken breast	1-1/2 lbs.	3 c., cooked and diced
Crumbs, bread	3 slices bread, torn	1 c.
Crumbs, graham cracker	14 graham crackers, crushed	1 c.
Crumbs, saltines	28 saltines, crushed	1 c.
Crumbs, vanilla wafer	22 vanilla wafers, crushed	1 c.
Garlic	1 clove	1/4 t., minced
Onions	1 large	1 c., chopped
Pasta	1 c., uncooked	2 to 3 c. cooked pasta
Potatoes	1 medium	1 c., chopped
Rice	1 c., uncooked	3 c. cooked rice
Tomatoes	1 large	1 c., chopped
Vegetables, frozen	10-oz. pkg.	2 c. fresh veggies, chopped
Vegetables, canned	16-oz. can	2 c. fresh veggies, chopped

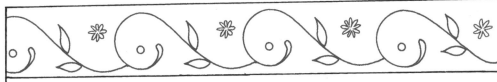

Seasoning Suggestions

Baked Goods	allspice, cinnamon, cloves, ginger, nutmeg
Beef	allspice, basil, bay, chili powder, curry powder, garlic, ginger, marjoram, pepper, oregano, thyme
Chicken	rosemary, sage, tarragon
Eggs	chives, dill weed, mustard, paprika, savory
Fish & Seafood	fennel, mustard, parsley, tarragon
Pork	caraway seed, chili powder, cumin, curry powder, dill, garlic, rosemary, sage, fennel, savory, thyme
Salads	basil, celery seed, chives, dill weed, parsley, tarragon
Soups & Stews	bay leaf, parsley, pepper, marjoram, thyme
Vegetables	chives, dill, ginger, marjoram, thyme
Beans	cumin, savory
Potatoes	caraway seed, paprika, rosemary
Tomatoes	basil, celery seed, oregano

Recipe Abbreviations

t. = teaspoon	ltr. = liter
T. = tablespoon	oz. = ounce
c. = cup	lb. = pound
pt. = pint	doz. = dozen
qt. = quart	pkg. = package
gal. = gallon	env. = envelope

Index

Index

Mains

Salads

Index

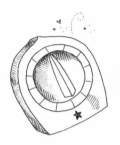

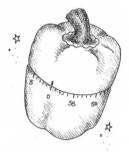

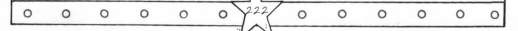

We've cooked up a whole collection of Gooseberry Patch® books!

Have a taste for more? Call us toll-free at
1-800-854-6673
We'll send you our latest catalog filled with kitchenware, candles, handmade quilts, gourmet goodies, enamelware, bowls, bubble night lights and our very own line of cookbooks, calendars and organizers!

Phone us:
1·800·854·6673

Fax us:
1·740·363·7225

Visit our website:
www.gooseberrypatch.com

Send us your favorite recipe!

and the memory that makes it special for you!* If we select your recipe for a brand new **Gooseberry Patch** cookbook, your name will appear right along with it...and you'll receive a FREE copy of the book! Mail to:

Gooseberry Patch
Attn: Book Dept.
P.O. Box 190
Delaware, OH 43015

*Please include the number of servings and all other necessary information!

U.S. to Canadian recipe equivalents

Volume Measurements

1/4 teaspoon	1 mL
1/2 teaspoon	2 mL
1 teaspoon	5 mL
1 tablespoon = 3 teaspoons	15 mL
2 tablespoons = 1 fluid ounce	30 mL
1/4 cup	60 mL
1/3 cup	75 mL
1/2 cup = 4 fluid ounces	125 mL
1 cup = 8 fluid ounces	250 mL
2 cups = 1 pint =16 fluid ounces	500 mL
4 cups = 1 quart	1 L

Weights

1 ounce	30 g
4 ounces	120 g
8 ounces	225 g
16 ounces = 1 pound	450 g

Oven Temperatures

300° F	150° C
325° F	160° C
350° F	180° C
375° F	190° C
400° F	200° C
450° F	230° C

Baking Pan Sizes

Square		Loaf	
8x8x2 inches	2 L = 20x20x5 cm	9x5x3 inches	2 L = 23x13x7 cm
9x9x2 inches	2.5 L = 23x23x5 cm	Round	
Rectangular		8x1-1/2 inches	1.2 L = 20x4 cm
13x9x2 inches	3.5 L = 33x23x5 cm	9x1-1/2 inches	1.5 L = 23x4 cm